Good Housekeeping

Kitchen Comforts

PAVILION

First published in the United Kingdom in 2014 by
Pavilion Books Company Limited
1 Gower Street
London
WC1E 6HD

The Good Housekeeping website is
www.goodhousekeeping.co.uk

10 9 8 7 6 5 4 3 2 1

ISBN 978-1-909397-96-5

A catalogue record for this book is available from the British Library.

Reproduction by Dot Gradations Ltd, UK
Printed and bound by Times Offset (M) Sdn Bhd, Malaysia

This book can be ordered direct from the publisher at www.pavilionbooks.com

Picture Credits
Photographers: Neil Barclay (pages 13,
28, 30, 36, 38, 62, 63, 65, 68, 70, 75, 87,
130, 132, 142 and 177); Martin Brigdale
(pages 108, 139, 140, 148, 160, 167, 204,
205, 206 and 207); Nicki Dowey (pages 8,
10, 11, 12, 14, 15, 17, 19, 20, 21, 22, 23,
24, 25, 29, 31, 33, 34, 35, 37, 39, 43, 44,
46, 47, 48, 50, 53, 54, 58, 59, 67, 85, 86,
88, 89, 95, 96, 99, 101, 103, 106, 107,
118, 120, 122, 125, 128, 131, 133, 143,
146, 147, 150, 151, 152, 153, 154, 156,
155, 166, 162, 165, 168, 169, 170, 181,
185, 187, 192, 193, 194, 196, 197, 200,
201, 202, 203, 210, 213, 216, 224, 236,
226, 227, 231, 232 and 234); Will Heap
(pages 41, 102, 124, 176, 191 and 199);
Craig Robertson (pages 16, 18, 32, 40,
57, 64, 69, 72, 76, 77, 78, 80, 82, 90,
91, 92, 94, 100, 104, 105, 107, 112,
114, 115, 117, 138, 144, 145, 158, 159,
164, 173, 179, 180, 182, 183, 184, 186,
190, 198, 211, 212, 214, 216, 217, 218,
220, 221, 222, 223, 225, 228, 233 and
237); Clive Streeter (pages 71 and 119);
Lucinda Symons (pages 52, 56, 66, 79,
116, 134, 141, 172, 178, 188, 195 and
230); Martin Thompson (page 74).

Home Economists: Anna Burges-Lumsden,
Joanna Farrow, Emma Jane Frost, Teresa
Goldfinch, Alice Hart, Lucy McKelvie, Kim
Morphew, Katie Rogers, Bridget Sargeson,
Jennifer White and Mari Mererid Williams.

Stylists: Lucy McKelvie, Helen Trent and
Fanny Ward.

Notes
Both metric and imperial measures are given for the recipes. Follow either set of
not a mixture of both, as they are not interchangeable.
All spoon measures are level.
1 tsp = 5ml spoon; 1 tbsp = 15ml spoon.
Ovens and grills must be preheated to the specified temperature.
Medium eggs should be used except where otherwise specified.

Dietary guidelines
Note that certain recipes contain raw or lightly cooked eggs. The young, elderly, pregnant
women and anyone with immune-deficiency disease should avoid these because of the
slight risk of salmonella.
Note that some recipes contain alcohol. Check the ingredients list before serving to children.

Contents

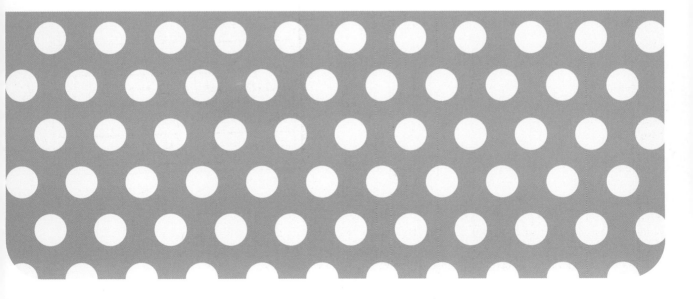

SOUPS

Chicken & Bean Soup

Preparation Time 10 minutes • Cooking Time 30 minutes • Serves 4 • Per Serving 351 calories, 6g fat (of which 1g saturates), 48g carbohydrate, 2.7g salt • Easy

1 tbsp olive oil

1 onion, finely chopped

4 celery sticks, chopped

1 red chilli, seeded and roughly chopped (see Cook's Tip, page 20)

2 boneless, skinless chicken breasts, about 125g (4oz) each, cut into strips

1 litre (1¾ pints) hot chicken or vegetable stock

100g (3½oz) bulgur wheat

2 × 400g cans cannellini beans, drained and rinsed

400g can chopped tomatoes

25g (1oz) flat-leafed parsley, roughly chopped

salt and ground black pepper

wholegrain bread and hummus to serve

1. Heat the oil in a large heavy-based pan. Add the onion, celery and chilli and cook over a low heat for 10 minutes or until softened. Add the chicken and stir-fry for 3–4 minutes until golden.

2. Add the hot stock to the pan and bring to a simmer. Stir in the bulgur wheat and simmer for 15 minutes.

3. Stir in the cannellini beans and tomatoes and bring to a simmer. Check the seasoning. Ladle into four warmed bowls and sprinkle with chopped parsley. Serve with wholegrain bread and hummus.

Mulligatawny Soup

Preparation Time 5 minutes • Cooking Time 40 minutes • Serves 4 • Per Serving 252 calories, 13g fat
(of which 4g saturates), 7g carbohydrate, 0.9g salt • Easy

**3 rashers streaky bacon, rinded
and finely chopped**
550g (1¼lb) chicken portions
600ml (1 pint) hot chicken stock
1 carrot, sliced
1 celery stick, chopped
1 apple, cored and chopped
2 tsp curry powder
4 peppercorns, crushed
1 clove
1 bay leaf
1 tbsp plain flour
150ml (¼ pint) milk
**50g (2oz) long-grain rice, cooked,
and crusty bread to serve**

1. Fry the bacon in a large pan until the fat begins to run. Do not allow the bacon to become brown.

2. Add the chicken and brown well. Drain the meat on kitchen paper and pour off the fat.

3. Return the bacon and chicken to the pan and add the hot stock and next seven ingredients. Cover the pan and simmer for about 30 minutes or until the chicken is tender.

4. Remove the chicken and allow to cool a little. Cut off the meat and return it to the soup. Discard the clove and bay leaf and reheat the soup gently.

5. Mix the flour with a little cold water. Add to the soup with the milk and reheat without boiling.

6. Ladle the soup into warmed bowls, spoon a mound of rice into each one and serve immediately with crusty bread.

Chicken Broth

Preparation Time 30 minutes • Cooking Time 15 minutes • Serves 4 • Per Serving 229 calories, 7g fat
(of which 1g saturates), 16g carbohydrate, 1.2g salt • Easy

1 tbsp olive oil

about 300g (11oz) boneless,
  skinless chicken thighs, cubed

3 garlic cloves, crushed

2 medium red chillies, seeded and
  finely diced (see Cook's Tip,
  page 20)

1 litre (1¾ pints) chicken stock

250g (9oz) each green beans,
  broccoli, sugarsnap peas and
  courgettes, chopped

50g (2oz) pasta shapes or spaghetti,
  broken into short lengths

salt and ground black pepper

1. Heat the oil in a large pan, add the chicken, garlic and chillies, and cook for 5–10 minutes until the chicken is opaque all over.

2. Add the stock and bring to the boil, then add the vegetables, reduce the heat and simmer for 5 minutes or until the chicken is cooked through.

3. Meanwhile, cook the pasta in a separate pan of lightly salted boiling water until just cooked – this will take 5–10 minutes, depending on the type of pasta.

4. Drain the pasta and add to the broth. Check the seasoning. Ladle into warmed bowls and serve immediately.

Hearty Chicken Soup with Dumplings

Preparation Time 20 minutes • Cooking Time 40 minutes • Serves 4 • Per Serving 335 calories, 15g fat (of which 5g saturates), 31g carbohydrate, 0.3g salt • Easy

2 tbsp olive oil
2 celery sticks, roughly chopped
150g (5oz) carrots, roughly chopped
150g (5oz) waxy salad potatoes,
   thinly sliced
275g (10oz) chicken breast,
   thinly sliced
2 litres (3½ pints) hot chicken stock
salt and ground black pepper
a handful of chives, roughly
   chopped, to garnish (optional)

FOR THE DUMPLINGS
100g (3½oz) plain flour
½ tsp baking powder
½ tsp salt
1 medium egg, well beaten
25g (1oz) butter, melted
a splash of milk

1. Heat the oil in a large pan, then add the celery, carrots and potatoes. Cook for 5 minutes or until the vegetables are beginning to caramelise around the edges. Add the chicken and fry for 3 minutes or until just starting to turn golden. Pour in the hot stock and simmer for 15 minutes, skimming the surface occasionally to remove any scum.

2. To make the dumplings, sift the flour, baking powder and salt into a bowl, then season with black pepper. Combine the egg, melted butter and milk in a separate bowl, then stir quickly into the flour to make a stiff batter.

3. Drop half-teaspoonfuls of the dumpling mixture into the soup, then cover and simmer for a further 15 minutes.

4. Check the seasoning, sprinkle with pepper and serve garnished with chives, if you like.

Cock-a-leekie Soup

Preparation Time 30–40 minutes • Cooking Time 1 hour 20 minutes, plus cooling • Serves 8 • Per Serving
280 calories, 4g fat (of which 1g saturates), 40g carbohydrate, 0.2g salt • Easy

**1 oven-ready chicken, about
   1.4kg (3lb)
2 onions, roughly chopped
2 carrots, roughly chopped
2 celery sticks, roughly chopped
1 bay leaf
25g (1oz) butter
900g (2lb) leeks, trimmed and
   sliced
125g (4oz) ready-to-eat dried
   prunes, sliced
salt and ground black pepper
freshly chopped parsley to serve**

**FOR THE DUMPLINGS
125g (4oz) self-raising flour
a pinch of salt
50g (2oz) shredded suet
2 tbsp freshly chopped parsley
2 tbsp freshly chopped thyme**

1. Put the chicken into a pan in which it fits quite snugly, then add the chopped vegetables, bay leaf and chicken giblets (if available). Pour in 1.7 litres (3 pints) water and bring to the boil, then reduce the heat, cover and simmer gently for 1 hour.

2. Meanwhile, melt the butter in a large pan, add the leeks and fry gently for 10 minutes or until softened.

3. Remove the chicken from the pan and leave until cool enough to handle. Strain the stock and put to one side. Strip the chicken from the bones and shred roughly. Add to the stock with the prunes and softened leeks.

4. To make the dumplings, sift the flour and salt into a bowl. Stir in the suet, herbs and about 5 tbsp water to make a fairly firm dough. Lightly shape the dough into 2.5cm (1in) balls. Bring the soup just to the boil and season well. Reduce the heat, add the dumplings and cover the pan with a lid. Simmer for 15–20 minutes until the dumplings are light and fluffy. Serve the soup scattered with chopped parsley.

COOK'S TIP
Make the stock a day ahead, if possible, then cool overnight. The following day, remove any fat from the surface.

Hot & Sour Soup

Preparation Time 20 minutes • Cooking Time 30–35 minutes • Serves 4 • Per Serving 255 calories, 10g fat (of which 1g saturates), 19g carbohydrate, 0.7g salt • Easy

1 tbsp vegetable oil

2 turkey breasts, about 300g (11oz), or the same quantity of tofu, cut into strips

5cm (2in) piece fresh root ginger, peeled and grated

4 spring onions, finely sliced

1–2 tbsp Thai red curry paste

75g (3oz) long-grain wild rice

1.1 litres (2 pints) hot weak chicken or vegetable stock, or boiling water

200g (7oz) mangetouts, sliced

juice of 1 lime

4 tbsp roughly chopped fresh coriander to garnish

1. Heat the oil in a deep pan. Add the turkey or tofu slices and cook over a medium heat for 5 minutes or until browned. Add the ginger and spring onions, and cook for a further 2–3 minutes. Stir in the curry paste and cook for 1–2 minutes to warm the spices.

2. Add the rice and stir to coat in the curry paste. Pour the hot stock or boiling water into the pan, stir once and bring to the boil. Reduce the heat, cover the pan and simmer for 20 minutes.

3. Add the mangetouts and cook for a further 5 minutes or until the rice is cooked. Just before serving, squeeze in the lime juice and stir to mix.

4. To serve, ladle into warmed bowls and sprinkle with the coriander.

Spiced Beef & Noodle Soup

Preparation Time 20 minutes • Cooking Time 15 minutes • Serves 4 • Per Serving 215 calories, 13g fat (of which 3g saturates), 11g carbohydrate, 1.2g salt • Easy

2 tbsp sunflower oil

225g (8oz) fillet steak, cut into thin strips

1.1 litres (2 pints) beef stock

2–3 tbsp Thai fish sauce (nam pla)

1 large red chilli, seeded and finely sliced (see Cook's Tip, page 20)

1 lemongrass stalk, trimmed and thinly sliced

2.5cm (1in) piece fresh root ginger, peeled and finely shredded

6 spring onions, halved lengthways and cut into 2.5cm (1in) lengths

1 garlic clove, crushed

¼ tsp caster sugar

15g (½oz) dried porcini or shiitake mushrooms, broken into pieces and soaked in 150ml (¼ pint) boiling water for 15 minutes

50g (2oz) medium egg noodles

125g (4oz) baby spinach leaves

4 tbsp fresh coriander leaves

salt and ground black pepper

1. Heat the oil in a large pan, then brown the meat in two batches and keep to one side.

2. Pour the stock into the pan with 2 tbsp of the fish sauce, the chilli, lemongrass, ginger, spring onions crushed garlic and sugar. Add the mushrooms and their soaking liquid. Bring the mixture to the boil.

3. Break up the noodles slightly and add them to the pan, then stir gently until they begin to separate. Reduce the heat and simmer the soup, stirring occasionally, for 4–5 minutes until the noodles are just tender.

4. Stir in the spinach, coriander and reserved beef. Season with salt and pepper, add the remaining fish sauce to taste, then serve the soup in warmed bowls.

Scotch Broth

Preparation Time 15 minutes • Cooking Time 2 hours • Serves 8 • Per Serving 173 calories, 2g fat
(of which trace saturates), 35g carbohydrate, 2.3g salt • Easy

1 piece marrow bone, about 350g (12oz)

1.4kg (3lb) piece beef skirt (ask your butcher for this)

300g (11oz) broth mix (to include pearl barley, red lentils, split peas and green peas), soaked according to the pack instructions

2 carrots, finely chopped

1 parsnip, finely chopped

2 onions, finely chopped

¼ white cabbage, finely chopped

1 leek, trimmed and finely chopped

½ tbsp salt

ground black pepper

2 tbsp freshly chopped parsley to serve

1. Put the marrow bone and beef skirt into a 5.7 litre (10 pint) stock pot and add 2.6 litres (4½ pints) cold water – there should be enough to cover the meat.

2. Bring the water to the boil. Remove any scum from the surface with a spoon and discard. Reduce the heat to low, add the broth mix and simmer, partially covered, for 1½ hours, skimming the surface occasionally if necessary.

3. Add the carrots, parsnip, onions, cabbage, leek and another 600ml (1 pint) cold water. Cover to bring to the boil quickly, then reduce the heat and simmer for 30 minutes.

4. Remove the marrow bone and piece of beef from the broth. Add a few shreds of beef to the broth, if you like. Season the broth well with the salt and some pepper and stir in the chopped parsley. Ladle into warmed bowls and serve hot.

COOK'S TIP

This is really two meals in one, a starter and a main course. The beef flavours the stock and is removed before serving. Later, you divide up the meat and serve it with mashed potatoes, swedes or turnips.

Parsnip Soup with Chorizo

Preparation Time 20 minutes • Cooking Time 1 hour • Serves 8 • Per Serving 278 calories, 20g fat (of which 9g saturates), 18g carbohydrate, 0.7g salt • Easy

40g (1½oz) butter

1 onion, roughly chopped

225g (8oz) floury potatoes such as King Edward, peeled and chopped

400g (14oz) parsnips, peeled and chopped

4 tsp paprika, plus extra to dust

1.1 litres (2 pints) vegetable stock

450ml (¾ pint) milk

4 tbsp double cream

75g (3oz) sliced chorizo sausage, cut into fine strips

salt and ground black pepper

parsnip crisps and freshly grated Parmesan to serve

1. Melt the butter in a large heavy-based pan over a gentle heat. Add the onion and cook for 5 minutes until soft. Add the potatoes, parsnips and paprika, mix well and cook gently, stirring occasionally, for 15 minutes or until the vegetables begin to soften.

2. Add the stock, milk and cream, and season with salt and pepper. Bring to the boil, then reduce the heat and simmer for 25 minutes or until the vegetables are very soft. Add 50g (2oz) of the chorizo. Allow the soup to cool a little, then whiz in a food processor or blender until smooth. The soup can be thinned with additional stock or milk, if you like. Check the seasoning and put back into the pan.

3. To serve, reheat the soup. Serve in warmed bowls and top each with parsnip crisps; sprinkle with the remaining chorizo and a little Parmesan and dust with paprika.

FREEZING TIP

To freeze Complete the recipe to the end of step 2, then cool, pack and freeze for up to one month. *To use* Thaw the soup overnight at cool room temperature, then complete the recipe.

Smoked Cod & Sweetcorn Chowder

Preparation Time 5 minutes • Cooking Time 20 minutes • Serves 6 • Per Serving 517 calories, 28g fat (of which 15g saturates), 35g carbohydrate, 4.7g salt • Easy

130g pack cubed pancetta

50g (2oz) butter

3 leeks, about 450g (1lb), trimmed and thinly sliced

25g (1oz) plain flour

600ml (1 pint) semi-skimmed or full-fat milk

700g (1½lb) undyed smoked cod loin or haddock, skinned and cut into 2cm (¾in) cubes

326g can sweetcorn in water, drained

450g (1lb) small new potatoes, sliced

150ml (¼ pint) double cream

½ tsp paprika

salt and ground black pepper

2 tbsp freshly chopped flat-leafed parsley to garnish

1. Fry the pancetta in a large pan over a gentle heat until the fat runs out. Add the butter to the pan to melt, then add the leeks and cook until softened.

2. Stir in the flour and cook for a few seconds, then pour in the milk and 300ml (½ pint) cold water. Add the fish to the pan with the sweetcorn and potatoes. Bring to the boil, then reduce the heat and simmer for 10–15 minutes until the potatoes are cooked.

3. Stir in the cream, season with salt and pepper and the paprika, and cook for 2–3 minutes to warm through. Ladle into warmed shallow bowls and sprinkle each one with a little chopped parsley. Serve immediately.

Autumn Barley Soup

Preparation Time 10 minutes • Cooking Time 1 hour 5 minutes • Serves 4 • Per Serving 83 calories, 1g fat (of which trace saturates), 16g carbohydrate, 0.6g salt • Vegetarian • Easy

25g (1oz) pot barley, washed
   and drained
1 litre (1¾ pints) hot vegetable
   stock
2 large carrots, diced
1 turnip, diced
2 leeks, trimmed and sliced
2 celery sticks, diced
1 small onion, finely chopped
1 bouquet garni (see Cook's Tip,
   page 22)
2 tbsp freshly chopped flat-leafed
   parsley
salt and ground black pepper

1. Put the barley and hot stock into a pan and bring to the boil. Reduce the heat and simmer for 45 minutes or until the barley is tender.

2. Add the vegetables to the pan with the bouquet garni and season to taste with salt and pepper. Bring to the boil, then reduce the heat and simmer for about 20 minutes or until the vegetables are tender.

3. Discard the bouquet garni. Add the parsley to the soup, stir well and serve immediately.

TRY SOMETHING DIFFERENT
Replace the barley with 75g (3oz) soup pasta: add for the last 10 minutes of cooking.

Cauliflower Soup

Preparation Time 25 minutes • Cooking Time 40 minutes • Serves 6 • Per Serving 115 calories, 7g fat (of which 1g saturates), 18g carbohydrate, 1g salt • Easy

2 × 400ml cans coconut milk
750ml (1¼ pints) vegetable stock
4 garlic cloves, finely chopped
5cm (2in) piece fresh root ginger, peeled and finely chopped
4 lemongrass stalks, roughly chopped
4 red chillies, seeded and chopped (see Cook's Tip)
4 kaffir lime leaves, shredded (optional)

2 tbsp groundnut oil
2 tsp sesame oil
1 large onion, thinly sliced
2 tsp ground turmeric
2 tsp sugar
900g (2lb) cauliflower florets
2 tbsp lime juice
2 tbsp light soy sauce
4 spring onions, shredded
4 tbsp freshly chopped coriander
salt and ground black pepper

1. Put the coconut milk and stock into a pan. Add the garlic and ginger with the lemongrass, chillies and lime leaves. Bring to the boil, then reduce the heat, cover the pan and simmer for 15 minutes. Strain and keep the liquid to one side.

2. Heat the oils together in a clean pan. Add the onion, turmeric and sugar, and fry gently for 5 minutes. Add the cauliflower to the pan and stir-fry for 5 minutes or until lightly golden.

3. Add the reserved liquid, the lime juice and soy sauce. Bring to the boil, then reduce the heat, cover the pan and simmer for 10–15 minutes until the cauliflower is tender. Season with salt and pepper, then divide among six warmed bowls. Scatter the spring onions and coriander on top and serve.

COOK'S TIP

Chillies vary enormously in strength, from quite mild to blisteringly hot, depending on the type of chilli and its ripeness. Taste a small piece first to check it's not too hot for you. Be extremely careful when handling chillies not to touch or rub your eyes with your fingers, as the oil in the chilli will sting. Wash knives immediately after handling chillies for the same reason. As a precaution, use rubber gloves when preparing them, if you like.

Full-of-goodness Broth

Preparation Time 10 minutes • Cooking Time 6–8 minutes • Serves 4 • Per Serving 107 calories, 4g fat (of which trace saturates), 9g carbohydrate, 1g salt • Vegetarian • Easy

1–2 tbsp medium curry paste (see Cook's Tip)
200ml (7fl oz) reduced-fat coconut milk
600ml (1 pint) hot vegetable stock
200g (7oz) smoked tofu, cubed
2 pak choi, chopped
a handful of sugarsnap peas
4 spring onions, chopped
lime wedges to serve

1. Heat the curry paste in a pan for 1–2 minutes. Add the coconut milk and hot stock, and bring to the boil.

2. Add the smoked tofu, pak choi, sugarsnap peas and spring onions. Reduce the heat and simmer for 1–2 minutes.

3. Ladle into warmed bowls and serve with a wedge of lime to squeeze over the broth.

TRY SOMETHING DIFFERENT
Replace the smoked tofu with shredded leftover roast chicken and simmer for 2–3 minutes.

COOK'S TIP
Check the ingredients in the curry paste: some may not be suitable for vegetarians.

French Onion Soup

Preparation Time 30 minutes • Cooking Time about 1 hour • Serves 4 • Per Serving 438 calories, 21g fat
(of which 13g saturates), 45g carbohydrate, 1.3g salt • Vegetarian • Easy

75g (3oz) butter
700g (1½lb) small onions, finely chopped
3 garlic cloves, crushed
1 tbsp plain flour
200ml (7fl oz) dry white wine (optional)
1.4 litres (2½ pints) vegetable stock
bouquet garni (see Cook's Tip)
salt and ground black pepper

TO SERVE
1 small baguette, cut into slices 1cm (½in) thick
50g (2oz) Gruyère or Cheddar cheese, grated (see Cook's Tips, page 177)

1. Melt the butter in a large heavy-based pan. Add the onions and cook slowly over a very low heat, stirring frequently, until very soft and golden brown; this should take at least 30 minutes. Add the garlic and flour and cook, stirring, for 1 minute.

2. Pour in the wine, if using, and let it bubble until reduced by half. Add the stock, bouquet garni and seasoning. Bring to the boil, then reduce the heat and simmer gently, uncovered, for 20–30 minutes.

3. Discard the bouquet garni and let the soup cool a little. Whiz one-third in a food processor or blender until smooth, then stir this back into the soup in the pan.

4. Preheat the grill. Lightly toast the baguette slices on both sides. Reheat the onion soup and adjust the seasoning.

5. Divide the soup among four ovenproof soup bowls. Float two or three slices of toast on each portion and sprinkle thickly with the grated cheese. Stand the bowls under the hot grill until the cheese has melted and turned golden brown. Serve at once.

COOK'S TIP
To make a bouquet garni, tie together a sprig each of thyme and parsley with a bay leaf and a piece of celery.

Quick Winter Minestrone

Preparation Time 10 minutes • Cooking Time 45 minutes • Serves 4 • Per Serving 334 calories, 11g fat
(of which 3g saturates), 47g carbohydrate, 1.5g salt • Easy

2 tbsp olive oil
1 small onion, finely chopped
1 carrot, chopped
1 celery stick, chopped
1 garlic clove, crushed
2 tbsp freshly chopped thyme
1 litre (1¾ pints) hot vegetable
    stock
400g can chopped tomatoes
400g can borlotti beans, drained
    and rinsed
125g (4oz) minestrone pasta
175g (6oz) Savoy cabbage, shredded
salt and ground black pepper
fresh Pesto (see Cook's Tip),
    toasted ciabatta and extra virgin
    olive oil to serve

COOK'S TIP

Pesto

Put a 20g pack of roughly chopped basil into a food processor. Add 25g (1oz) finely grated Parmesan, 50g (2oz) pinenuts and 4 tbsp extra virgin olive oil and whiz to a rough paste. Alternatively, grind in a pestle and mortar. Season with salt and plenty of ground black pepper.

1. Heat the oil in a large pan and add the onion, carrot and celery. Cook for 8–10 minutes until softened, then add the garlic and thyme and fry for another 2–3 minutes.

2. Add the hot stock, tomatoes and half the borlotti beans to the pan and bring to the boil. Mash the remaining beans and stir into the soup, then reduce the heat and simmer for 30 minutes, adding the minestrone pasta and cabbage for the last 10 minutes of cooking time.

3. Check the seasoning, then ladle the soup into four warmed bowls and serve with a dollop of fresh pesto on top and slices of toasted ciabatta drizzled with extra virgin olive oil on the side.

Mixed Mushroom Soup

Preparation Time • 15 minutes, plus soaking • Cooking Time 35 minutes • Serves 4 • Per Serving 158 calories,
12g fat (of which 2g saturates), 10g carbohydrate, 0.2g salt • Easy

15g (½oz) dried porcini mushrooms
1 tbsp sunflower oil, plus 50ml
(2fl oz) to shallow-fry
1 small onion, chopped
450g (1lb) chestnut mushrooms,
chopped
600ml (1 pint) hot vegetable stock
2 slices white bread, crusts
removed, cut into cubes
2 garlic cloves, finely sliced
salt and ground black pepper
freshly chopped flat-leafed parsley
to garnish
a drizzle of cream to serve

1. Put the porcini into a bowl, pour over 75ml (2½fl oz) boiling water and leave to soak for 10 minutes. Strain the porcini, put the liquid to one side, then chop roughly, keeping 1 tbsp to use as a garnish.

2. Heat 1 tbsp oil in a pan. Add the onion and porcini, and cook over a medium heat for 5 minutes. Add the chestnut mushrooms, increase the heat and brown lightly for 5 minutes. Add the reserved porcini liquid and the hot stock, then bring to the boil.

Season well with salt and pepper and simmer for 20 minutes.

3. To make croûtons, heat 50ml (2fl oz) oil in a frying pan. Add the bread and garlic, and stir-fry for 2 minutes until golden. Drain on kitchen paper.

4. Take the soup off the heat and leave to cool slightly. Purée in a food processor or blender until smooth, then transfer to a clean pan. Reheat gently, then divide among four warmed bowls. Top with the croûtons, reserved porcini and a sprinkling of parsley, then drizzle with cream and serve.

Spinach & Rice Soup

Preparation Time 10 minutes • Cooking Time 25–30 minutes • Serves 4 • Per Serving 335 calories, 20g fat (of which 4g saturates), 29g carbohydrate, 0.7g salt • Vegetarian • Easy

4 tbsp extra virgin olive oil, plus
   extra to serve
1 onion, finely chopped
2 garlic cloves, crushed
2 tsp freshly chopped thyme or
   a large pinch of dried thyme
2 tsp freshly chopped rosemary or
   a large pinch of dried rosemary
zest of ½ lemon
2 tsp ground coriander

¼ tsp cayenne pepper
125g (4oz) arborio rice
1.1 litres (2 pints) vegetable stock
225g (8oz) fresh or frozen and
   thawed spinach, shredded
4 tbsp fresh Pesto (see Cook's Tip,
   page 23)
salt and ground black pepper
freshly grated Parmesan to serve
   (see Cook's Tips, page 177)

1. Heat half the oil in a pan. Add the onion, garlic, herbs, lemon zest and spices, then fry gently for 5 minutes.

2. Add the remaining oil with the rice and cook, stirring, for 1 minute. Add the stock and bring to the boil, then reduce the heat and simmer gently for 20 minutes or until the rice is tender.

3. Stir the spinach into the soup with the pesto. Cook for 2 minutes, then season to taste with salt and pepper.

4. Ladle into warmed bowls and serve drizzled with a little oil and topped with Parmesan.

PASTA &
RISOTTO

Chicken, Bacon & Leek Pasta Bake

Preparation Time 10 minutes • Cooking Time about 20 minutes • Serves 4 • Per Serving 650 calories, 24g fat (of which 6g saturates), 68g carbohydrate, 2.2g salt • Easy

1 tbsp olive oil
100g (3½oz) bacon lardons
450g (1lb) boneless, skinless chicken thighs, chopped
3 medium leeks, trimmed and chopped
300g (11oz) macaroni or other pasta shapes
350g carton ready-made cheese sauce
2 tsp Dijon mustard
2 tbsp freshly chopped flat-leafed parsley, plus extra to garnish
25g (1oz) freshly grated Parmesan
salt

1. Heat the oil in a large frying pan. Add the bacon and chicken, and cook for 7–8 minutes. Add the leeks and continue cooking for 4–5 minutes.

2. Meanwhile, cook the pasta in a large pan of lightly salted boiling water according to the pack instructions. Drain well.

3. Preheat the grill. Add the cheese sauce to the pasta with the mustard, chicken mixture and parsley. Mix well, then tip into a 2.1 litre (3¾ pint) ovenproof dish and sprinkle with Parmesan. Grill for 4–5 minutes until golden. Garnish with chopped parsley.

Pasta with Chicken, Cream & Basil

Preparation Time 10 minutes • Cooking Time 25 minutes • Serves 4 • Per Serving 612 calories, 27g fat
(of which 12g saturates), 67g carbohydrate, 0.4g salt • Easy

1 tbsp olive oil

2 shallots, chopped

400g (14oz) boneless chicken,
   cubed

125g (4oz) chestnut mushrooms,
   sliced

50g (2oz) sultanas

a pinch of ground cinnamon

50ml (2fl oz) dry white wine

125ml (4fl oz) hot chicken stock

300g (11oz) farfalle pasta

142ml carton double cream

2 tsp Dijon mustard

2 tsp freshly chopped basil

salt

1. Heat the oil in a pan. Add the
shallots and fry for 4–5 minutes.
Add the chicken and cook until
browned. Add the mushrooms
and cook for 2 minutes. Stir in
the sultanas and cinnamon.

2. Pour in the wine and hot stock
and simmer for 12–15 minutes
until the chicken is cooked.

3. While the sauce is cooking, cook
the pasta in a large pan of lightly
salted boiling water according to
the pack instructions.

4. Stir the cream, mustard and
basil into the chicken and season
with salt. Drain the pasta and return
to the pan, then add the sauce, toss
and serve.

Creamy Parma Ham & Artichoke Tagliatelle

Preparation Time 5 minutes • Cooking Time 12 minutes • Serves 4 • Per Serving 972 calories, 56g fat (of which 36g saturates), 97g carbohydrate, 1.1g salt • Easy

500g (1lb 2oz) tagliatelle

500ml (18fl oz) crème fraîche

280g jar roasted artichoke hearts, drained and each cut in half

80g pack Parma ham (6 slices), torn into strips

2 tbsp freshly chopped sage leaves, plus extra to garnish

salt and ground black pepper

40g (1½oz) Parmesan shavings to serve (see Cook's Tip)

1. Cook the pasta in a large pan of lightly salted boiling water according to the pack instructions.

2. Drain the pasta well, leaving a ladleful of the cooking water in the pan, then put the pasta back into the pan.

3. Add the crème fraîche to the pan with the artichoke hearts, Parma ham and sage, then stir everything together. Season well.

4. Spoon the pasta into warmed bowls, sprinkle with the Parmesan shavings and garnish with sage. Serve immediately.

COOK'S TIP

Make Parmesan shavings with a vegetable peeler. Hold the piece of cheese in one hand, and pare off wafer-thin strips of cheese using the peeler.

Spiced Pork with Lemon Pasta

Preparation Time 10 minutes • Cooking Time 12 minutes • Serves 6 • Per Serving 733 calories, 44g fat (of which 28g saturates), 71g carbohydrate, 1.8g salt • Easy

8 thick pork sausages

500g (1lb 2oz) pasta shells or other shapes

100ml (3½fl oz) chicken stock

grated zest of 1 lemon

juice of ½ lemon

a large pinch of dried chilli flakes

300ml (½ pint) half-fat crème fraîche

2 tbsp freshly chopped flat-leafed parsley, plus extra to garnish

salt and ground black pepper

25g (1oz) freshly grated Parmesan to serve

1. Remove the skin from the sausages and pinch the meat into small pieces. Heat a non-stick frying pan over a medium heat. When hot, add the sausagemeat and cook for 5 minutes, stirring occasionally, or until cooked through and browned.

2. Meanwhile, cook the pasta in a large pan of lightly salted boiling water according to the pack instructions until al dente.

3. Add the stock to the pan with the sausagemeat, bring to the boil and let it bubble, stirring, for 2–3 minutes until the liquid has reduced right down. Add the lemon zest and juice, chilli flakes and crème fraîche. Season well with salt and pepper. Continue to cook for 3–4 minutes until reduced and thickened slightly.

4. Drain the pasta and return to the pan. Stir the parsley into the sauce and toss with the pasta. Serve immediately, with grated Parmesan and a garnish of parsley.

Spicy Sausage & Pasta Supper

Preparation Time 15 minutes • Cooking Time 30 minutes • Serves 6 • Per Serving 629 calories, 39g fat
(of which 18g saturates), 36g carbohydrate, 3.1g salt • Easy

1 tbsp olive oil
200g (7oz) salami, sliced
225g (8oz) onion, finely chopped
50g (2oz) celery, finely chopped
2 garlic cloves, crushed
400g can pimientos, drained,
    rinsed and chopped
400g (14oz) passata or 400g can
    chopped tomatoes
125g (4oz) sun-dried tomatoes in
    oil, drained
600ml (1 pint) hot chicken or
    vegetable stock
300ml (½ pint) red wine
1 tbsp sugar
75g (3oz) dried pasta shapes

400g can borlotti beans, drained
    and rinsed
salt and ground black pepper
freshly chopped flat-leafed parsley
    to garnish
300ml (½ pint) soured cream and
    175g (6oz) Parmesan, freshly
    grated, to serve

1. Heat the oil in a large pan over a medium heat and fry the salami for 5 minutes or until golden and crisp. Drain on kitchen paper.

2. Fry the onion and celery in the hot oil for 10 minutes or until soft and golden. Add the garlic and fry for 1 minute. Put the salami back into the pan with the pimientos, passata or chopped tomatoes, the sun-dried tomatoes, hot stock, wine and sugar. Bring to the boil.

3. Stir in the pasta, bring back to the boil and cook for about 10 minutes, or according to the pack instructions, until the pasta is almost tender.

4. Stir in the beans and simmer for 3–4 minutes. Top up with more hot stock if the pasta is not tender when the liquid has been absorbed. Season with salt and pepper.

5. Ladle into warmed bowls and serve topped with soured cream and garnished with chopped parsley. Serve the grated Parmesan separately.

GET AHEAD

To prepare ahead *Complete the recipe to the end of step 2. Cool quickly, cover and chill for up to one day.*
To use *Bring back to the boil, stir in the pasta and complete the recipe.*

Stuffed Pasta Shells

Preparation Time 15 minutes • Cooking Time about 1 hour • Serves 6 • Per Serving 378 calories, 17g fat (of which 5g saturates), 41g carbohydrate, 1.1g salt • Easy

2 tbsp olive oil

1 large onion, finely chopped

a few fresh rosemary or oregano sprigs, chopped

125g (4oz) small flat mushrooms, sliced

6 plump coarse sausages, skinned

175ml (6fl oz) red wine

300ml (½ pint) passata

4 tbsp sun-dried tomato paste

sugar to taste, if necessary

250g (9oz) large pasta shells, such as conchiglioni rigati

150ml (¼ pint) half-fat single cream (optional)

freshly grated Parmesan to garnish

green salad to serve

1. Preheat the oven to 180°C (160°C fan oven) mark 4 Heat the oil in a deep frying pan. Stir in the onion and rosemary or oregano and cook over a gentle heat for 10 minutes or until the onion is soft and golden. Add the mushrooms and cook over a medium heat until the vegetables are soft and beginning to brown at the edges. Tip the onion mixture into a bowl.

2. Crumble the sausagemeat into the hot pan and stir over a high heat with a wooden spoon, breaking the meat up as you do so, until browned all over. Reduce the heat slightly and pour in the wine. Leave to bubble and reduce by about half. Return the onion mixture to the pan and add the passata and sun-dried tomato paste. Bubble gently for another 10 minutes. Add a pinch of sugar if the sauce tastes a little sharp.

3. While the sauce is simmering, cook the pasta shells in plenty of boiling water for 10 minutes or until just tender. Drain well and run under the cold tap to cool.

4. Fill the shells with the sauce and put into a shallow ovenproof dish. Drizzle with any extra sauce and the cream, if using, and bake for 30 minutes or until piping hot. Sprinkle with Parmesan and serve with a big bowl of green salad.

TRY SOMETHING DIFFERENT
• *Turkey or chicken mince would make a lighter alternative to the sausages: you will need 450g (1lb).*
• *Use a small aubergine, diced, instead of the mushrooms.*

Quick & Easy Carbonara

Preparation Time 5 minutes • Cooking Time 10 minutes • Serves 4 • Per Serving 688 calories, 39g fat
(of which 19g saturates), 65g carbohydrate, 1.6g salt • Easy

350g (12oz) tagliatelle
150g (5oz) smoked bacon, chopped
1 tbsp olive oil
2 large egg yolks
150ml (¼ pint) double cream
50g (2oz) freshly grated Parmesan
2 tbsp freshly chopped parsley

1. Cook the pasta in a large pan of lightly salted boiling water according to the pack instructions. Drain well.

2. Meanwhile, fry the bacon in the oil for 4–5 minutes. Add to the drained pasta and keep hot.

3. Put the egg yolks into a bowl, add the cream and whisk together. Add to the pasta with the Parmesan and parsley, toss well and serve.

Italian Meatballs

Preparation Time 15 minutes • Cooking Time 50 minutes • Serves 4 • Per Serving 275 calories, 12g fat (of which 4g saturates), 16g carbohydrate, 1.8g salt • Easy

50g (2oz) fresh breadcrumbs
450g (1lb) minced lean pork
1 tsp fennel seeds, crushed
¼ tsp dried chilli flakes, or to taste
3 garlic cloves, crushed
4 tbsp freshly chopped flat-leafed
    parsley
3 tbsp red wine
oil-water spray (see Cook's Tip)
roughly chopped fresh oregano
    to garnish
spaghetti to serve

FOR THE TOMATO SAUCE
oil-water spray
2 large shallots, finely chopped
3 pitted black olives, shredded
2 garlic cloves, crushed
2 pinches of dried chilli flakes
250ml (9fl oz) vegetable or
    chicken stock
500g carton passata
2 tbsp each freshly chopped flat-
    leafed parsley, basil and oregano
salt and ground black pepper

1. To make the tomato sauce, spray a pan with the oil-water spray and add the shallots. Cook gently for 5 minutes. Add the olives, garlic, chilli flakes and stock, and bring to the boil, then reduce the heat, cover and simmer for 3–4 minutes.

2. Uncover and simmer for 10 minutes or until the shallots and garlic are soft and the liquid syrupy. Stir in the passata and season with salt and pepper. Bring to the boil, then reduce the heat and simmer for 10–15 minutes. Stir in the herbs.

3. Meanwhile, put the breadcrumbs, pork, fennel seeds, chilli flakes, garlic, parsley and wine into a large bowl, season and mix together, using your hands, until thoroughly combined. (If you wish to check the seasoning, fry a little mixture, taste and adjust if necessary.)

4. With wet hands, roll the mixture into balls. Line a grill pan with foil, shiny side up, and spray with the oil-water spray. Cook the meatballs under a preheated grill

for 3–4 minutes on each side. Serve with the tomato sauce and spaghetti, garnished with oregano.

COOK'S TIP
Oil-water spray is far lower in calories than oil alone and, as it sprays on thinly and evenly, you'll use less. Fill one-eighth of a travel-sized spray bottle with oil such as sunflower, light olive or vegetable (rapeseed) oil, then top up with water. To use, shake well before spraying. Store in the fridge.

Chunky One-pot Bolognese

Preparation Time 15 minutes • Cooking Time about 1 hour • Serves 6 • Per Serving 506 calories, 31g fat (of which 11g saturates), 40g carbohydrate, 1.5g salt • Easy

3 tbsp olive oil
2 large red onions, finely diced
a few fresh rosemary sprigs
1 large aubergine, finely diced
8 plump coarse sausages
350ml (12fl oz) full-bodied red wine
700g (1½lb) passata
4 tbsp sun-dried tomato paste
300ml (½ pint) hot vegetable stock
175g (6oz) small pasta, such as orecchiette
salt and ground black pepper

1. Heat 2 tbsp oil in a large shallow non-stick pan. Add the onions and rosemary and cook over a gentle heat for 10 minutes or until soft and golden.

2. Add the aubergine and remaining oil and cook over a medium heat for 8–10 minutes until soft and golden.

3. Meanwhile, pull the skin off the sausages and divide each into four rough chunks. Tip the aubergine mixture on to a plate and add the sausage chunks to the hot pan. You won't need any extra oil.

4. Stir the sausage pieces over a high heat for 6–8 minutes until golden and beginning to turn crisp at the edges. Pour in the wine and let it bubble for 6–8 minutes until only a little liquid remains. Put the aubergine mixture back into the pan, along with the passata, tomato paste and hot stock.

5. Stir the pasta into the liquid and cover the pan, then simmer for 20 minutes or until the pasta is cooked. Taste and season with salt and pepper if necessary.

FREEZING TIP
To freeze Complete the recipe to the end of step 4. Add the 10 minutes – it will continue to cook right through when you reheat the Bolognese. Cool, put into a freezerproof container and freeze for up to three months.
To use Thaw overnight at cool room temperature, put into a pan and add 150ml (¼ pint) water. Bring to the boil, then simmer gently for 10 minutes or until the sauce is hot and the pasta is cooked.

Chilli Bolognese

Preparation Time 15 minutes • Cooking Time 30–40 minutes • Serves 4 • Per Serving 756 calories, 33g fat
(of which 13g saturates), 74g carbohydrate, 1.4g salt • Easy

1 tbsp olive oil
1 large onion, finely chopped
½ large red chilli, seeded and
    thinly sliced (see Cook's Tip,
    page 20)
450g (1lb) minced beef or lamb
125g (4oz) smoked bacon, rind
    removed, cut into strips
3 roasted red peppers, drained
    and finely chopped

400g can chopped tomatoes
125ml (4fl oz) red wine
300g (11oz) spaghetti
25g (1oz) freshly grated Cheddar
    or Gruyère cheese, plus extra
    to garnish
2 tbsp freshly chopped flat-leafed
    parsley (optional), plus extra
    to garnish
salt and ground black pepper

1. Heat the oil in a large pan over a medium heat. Add the onion and chilli, and fry for 5–10 minutes until soft and golden. Add the beef or lamb and the bacon strips, and stir over the heat for 5–7 minutes until well browned.

2. Stir in the red peppers, tomatoes and wine. Season with salt and pepper and bring to the boil, then reduce the heat and simmer over a low heat for 15–20 minutes.

3. Meanwhile, cook the pasta in a large pan of lightly salted boiling water according to the pack instructions. Drain.

4. Just before serving, stir the grated cheese, parsley, if using, and the sauce into the spaghetti. Garnish with extra grated cheese and chopped parsley.

Tagliatelle Bake

Preparation Time 5 minutes • Cooking Time 45 minutes • Serves 4 • Per Serving 935 calories, 42g fat (of which 19g saturates), 97g carbohydrate, 1.6g salt • Easy

1 tbsp olive oil
1 large onion, finely chopped
450g (1lb) minced beef
2 garlic cloves, crushed
290g jar marinated vegetables
2 × 400g cans chopped tomatoes
1 tsp dried marjoram
375g (13oz) fresh garlic and herb
   tagliatelle
330g jar ready-made cheese sauce
4 tbsp milk
75g (3oz) Cheddar cheese, grated
salt
mixed salad to serve

1. Heat the oil in a pan. Add the onion and fry until soft. Add the beef and fry, stirring, until the meat is brown. Add the garlic, vegetables, tomatoes and marjoram. Simmer for 25 minutes or until the meat is tender.

2. Cook the tagliatelle in a pan of lightly salted boiling water according to the pack instructions. Drain, put back into the pan and stir in the cheese sauce and milk. Heat through for 3 minutes.

3. Preheat the grill. Put alternate layers of mince and pasta into a heatproof dish, finishing with the pasta. Top with the cheese. Cook under the hot grill until bubbling. Serve with a mixed salad.

FREEZING TIP

To freeze Double the quantities and make another meal for four or make two meals for two people and freeze. Complete the recipe to the end of step 2, then layer the mince and pasta in a freezerproof, heatproof container. Cool and freeze for up to three months.
To use Thaw overnight in the fridge. Bake in the oven at 190°C (170°C fan oven) mark 5 for 25 minutes, then slide under a hot grill for 2–3 minutes until bubbling and lightly golden. Alternatively, make double the meat mixture, freeze half and serve with spaghetti or flour tortillas.

Greek Pasta Bake

Preparation Time 10 minutes • Cooking Time about 1½ hours • Serves 4 • Per Serving 736 calories, 30g fat (of which 13g saturates), 80g carbohydrate, 0.8g salt • Easy

2 tbsp vegetable oil
1 onion, finely chopped
2 garlic cloves, crushed
450g (1lb) extra-lean minced lamb
2 tbsp tomato purée
400g can chopped tomatoes
2 bay leaves
150ml (¼ pint) hot beef stock
350g (12oz) macaroni
50g (2oz) Cheddar cheese, grated
salt and ground black pepper

FOR THE SAUCE
15g (½oz) butter
15g (½oz) plain flour
300ml (½ pint) milk
1 medium egg, beaten

1. Heat the oil in a large pan, add the onion and garlic, and cook for 5 minutes to soften. Add the lamb and stir-fry over a high heat for 3–4 minutes until browned all over.

2. Stir in the tomato purée and cook for 1–2 minutes. Stir in the tomatoes, bay leaves and hot stock, and season with salt and pepper. Bring to the boil, then reduce the heat and cook for 35–40 minutes.

3. Meanwhile, make the sauce. Melt the butter in a small pan, then stir in the flour and cook over a medium heat for 1–2 minutes. Gradually add the milk, stirring constantly. Reduce the heat to low and cook, stirring, for 4–5 minutes. Remove from the heat and cool slightly. Stir in the beaten egg and season well with salt and pepper. Put to one side.

4. Preheat the oven to 180°C (160°C fan oven) mark 4. Cook the macaroni in a large pan of lightly salted boiling water according to the pack instructions until al dente.

5. Drain the pasta well and spoon half into a 2 litre (3½ pint) ovenproof dish. Spoon the meat mixture over it, then top with the remaining macaroni. Pour the sauce evenly over the top and scatter with the grated cheese. Cook in the oven for 25–30 minutes until golden.

Lamb & Pasta Pot

Preparation Time 10 minutes • Cooking Time 50 minutes • Serves 4 • Per Serving 686 calories, 36g fat
(of which 16g saturates), 18g carbohydrate, 1.4g salt • Easy

**1 half leg of lamb roasting joint –
  about 1.1kg (2½lb) total weight**
**125g (4oz) smoked streaky bacon,
  chopped**
150ml (¼ pint) red wine
**400g can chopped tomatoes with
  chilli, or 400g (14oz) passata**
75g (3oz) pasta shapes
12 sunblush tomatoes
**150g (5oz) chargrilled artichokes in
  oil, drained and halved**
a handful of basil leaves to garnish

1. Preheat the oven to 200°C (180°C fan oven) mark 6. Put the lamb and bacon into a small deep roasting tin and fry for 5 minutes or until the lamb is brown all over and the bacon is beginning to crisp.

2. Remove the lamb and put to one side. Pour the wine into the tin with the bacon – it should bubble immediately. Stir well, scraping the base to loosen any crusty bits, then leave to bubble until half the wine has evaporated. Stir in 300ml (½ pint) water and add the chopped tomatoes or passata, the pasta and sunblush tomatoes.

3. Put the lamb on a rack over the roasting tin so that the juices drip into the pasta. Cook, uncovered, in the oven for about 35 minutes.

4. Stir the artichokes into the pasta and put everything back in the oven for 5 minutes or until the lamb is tender and the pasta cooked. Slice the lamb thickly and serve with the pasta, garnished with the basil.

Steak with Onions & Tagliatelle

Preparation Time 10 minutes • Cooking Time 20 minutes • Serves 4 • Per Serving 557 calories, 26g fat
(of which 16g saturates), 51g carbohydrate, 0.2g salt • Easy

225g (8oz) tagliatelle
2 × 200g (7oz) sirloin steaks
2 red onions, thinly sliced
200g (7oz) low-fat crème fraîche
2 tbsp freshly chopped flat-leafed
  parsley
salt and ground black pepper

1. Cook the pasta in a large pan of lightly salted boiling water according to the pack instructions; do not overcook – it should be al dente. Drain well.

2. Meanwhile, season the steaks on both sides with salt and pepper. Heat a non-stick frying pan until really hot and fry the steaks for 2–3 minutes on each side until brown but still pink inside. Remove from the pan and set aside.

3. Add the onions to the pan and stir-fry for 8–10 minutes until softened and golden. Add a little water if they're sticking. Season, reduce the heat and stir in the crème fraîche.

4. Cut the fat off the steaks and discard, then cut the meat into thin strips. Add to the pan and cook briskly for 1–2 minutes, then stir in the pasta. Add the parsley, toss again and serve immediately.

Classic Lasagne

Preparation Time about 1 hour • Cooking Time 1 hour 20 minutes • Serves 6 • Per Serving 326 calories, 13g fat (of which 6g saturates), 37g carbohydrate, 0.5g salt • Easy

butter to grease

350g (12oz) fresh lasagne, or 225g (8oz) 'no need to pre-cook' lasagne (12–15 sheets, see Cook's Tip)

3 tbsp freshly grated Parmesan

salad to serve

FOR THE BOLOGNESE SAUCE

2 tbsp olive oil

1 onion, finely chopped

2 garlic cloves, crushed

450g (1lb) extra-lean minced beef

2 tbsp sun-dried tomato paste

300ml (½ pint) red wine

400g can chopped tomatoes

125g (4oz) chestnut mushrooms, sliced

2 tbsp Worcestershire sauce

salt and ground black pepper

FOR THE BÉCHAMEL SAUCE

300ml (½ pint) semi-skimmed milk

1 onion slice

6 peppercorns

1 mace blade

1 bay leaf

15g (½oz) butter

15g (½oz) plain flour

freshly grated nutmeg

salt and ground black pepper

1. To make the Bolognese sauce, heat the oil in a large pan, add the onion and fry over a medium heat for 10 minutes or until softened and golden. Add the garlic and cook for 1 minute. Add the beef and brown evenly, using a wooden spoon to break up the pieces. Stir in the tomato paste and wine, cover and bring to the boil. Add the tomatoes, mushrooms and Worcestershire sauce and season well with salt and pepper. Bring back to the boil, reduce the heat and simmer for 20 minutes.

2. Meanwhile, to make the béchamel sauce, pour the milk into a pan and add the onion, peppercorns, mace and bay leaf. Bring almost to the boil, then remove from the heat, cover and leave to infuse for about 20 minutes. Strain. Melt the butter in a pan, stir in the flour and cook, stirring, for 1 minute or until cooked but not coloured. Remove from the heat and gradually pour in the milk, whisking constantly. Season lightly with nutmeg, salt and pepper. Return to the heat and cook, stirring constantly, until the sauce is thickened and smooth. Simmer gently for 2 minutes.

3. Preheat the oven to 180°C (160°C fan oven) mark 4. Spoon one-third of the Bolognese sauce over the base of a greased 2.3 litre (4 pint) ovenproof dish. Cover with a layer of lasagne sheets, then a layer of béchamel. Repeat these layers twice more, finishing with a layer of béchamel to cover the lasagne.

4. Sprinkle the Parmesan over the top and stand the dish on a baking sheet. Cook in the oven for 45 minutes or until well browned and bubbling. Serve with salad.

COOK'S TIP

If using 'no need to pre-cook' lasagne, add a little extra stock or water to the sauce.

Cannelloni with Roasted Garlic

Preparation Time 40 minutes • Cooking Time about 1 hour • Serves 6 • Per serving 430 calories, 20g fat
(of which 9g saturates), 29g carbohydrate, 1.1g salt • A Little Effort

20 garlic cloves, unpeeled

2 tbsp extra virgin olive oil

**15g (½oz) dried porcini
mushrooms, soaked for
20 minutes in 150ml (¼ pint)
boiling water**

**5 shallots or button onions,
finely chopped**

700g (1½lb) lean minced meat

175ml (6fl oz) beef or lamb stock

2 tbsp freshly chopped thyme

about 12 lasagne sheets

**142ml carton single cream
mixed with 2 tbsp sun-dried
tomato paste**

butter to grease

**75g (3oz) Gruyère cheese,
finely grated**

salt and ground black pepper

1. Preheat the oven to 180°C (160°C fan oven) mark 4. Put the garlic into a small roasting tin with 1 tbsp oil. Toss to coat the garlic in the oil and cook for 25 minutes or until soft. Leave to cool.

2. Meanwhile, drain the porcini mushrooms, putting the liquor to one side, then rinse to remove any grit. Chop the mushrooms finely.

3. Heat the remaining oil in a pan. Add the shallots and cook over a medium heat for 5 minutes or until soft. Increase the heat and stir in the meat. Cook, stirring frequently, until browned. Add the stock, the mushrooms, with their liquor, and the thyme. Cook over a medium heat for 15–20 minutes until the liquid has almost evaporated. The mixture should be quite moist. Peel the garlic cloves and mash them to a rough paste with a fork. Stir into the meat mixture, then season with salt and pepper, and set aside.

4. Cook the lasagne according to the pack instructions until al dente. Drain, rinse with cold water and drain again. Lay each lasagne sheet on a clean teatowel. Spoon the meat mixture along one long edge and roll up to enclose the filling. Cut the tubes in half.

5. Season the cream and sun-dried tomato paste mixture. Preheat the oven to 200°C (180°C fan oven) mark 6. Grease a shallow baking dish. Arrange a layer of filled tubes in the base of the dish. Spoon half the tomato cream over them and sprinkle with half the cheese. Arrange the remaining tubes on top and cover with the remaining tomato cream and cheese. Cover the dish with foil and cook in the oven for 10 minutes. Uncover and cook for a further 5–10 minutes until lightly browned, then serve.

Seafood Spaghetti with Pepper & Almond Sauce

Preparation Time 20 minutes • Cooking Time 25 minutes • Serves 4 • Per Serving 426 calories, 9g fat (of which 1g saturates), 62g carbohydrate, 0.9g salt • Easy

1 small red pepper
1 red chilli (see Cook's Tip, page 20)
50g (2oz) blanched almonds
2–3 garlic cloves, chopped
2 tbsp red wine vinegar
350ml (12fl oz) tomato juice
a small handful of flat-leafed parsley
300g (11oz) spaghetti
450g (1lb) mixed cooked seafood, such as prawns, mussels and squid
salt and ground black pepper

1. Preheat the grill. Grill the red pepper and chilli, turning occasionally, until the skins char and blacken. Cover and leave to cool slightly, then peel off the skins. Halve, discard the seeds, then put the flesh into a food processor.

2. Toast the almonds under the grill until golden. Add the toasted almonds and garlic to the processor with the vinegar, tomato juice and half the parsley, then season with salt and pepper. Whiz until almost smooth, then transfer the sauce to a large pan.

3. Meanwhile, cook the spaghetti in a pan of lightly salted boiling water according to the pack instructions; keep it al dente.

4. Heat the sauce gently until it simmers, then add the seafood. Simmer for 3–4 minutes until the sauce and seafood have heated through, stirring frequently.

5. Roughly chop the remaining parsley. Drain the pasta and return to the pan, then add the sauce together with the parsley and toss well.

Pasta with Vegetables, Pinenuts & Pesto

Preparation Time 5 minutes • Cooking Time 15 minutes • Serves 4 • Per Serving 556 calories, 27g fat (of which 6g saturates), 60g carbohydrate, 0.5g salt • Vegetarian • Easy

300g (11oz) penne pasta
50g (2oz) pinenuts
1 tbsp olive oil
1 garlic clove, crushed
250g (9oz) closed-cup mushrooms, sliced
2 courgettes, sliced
250g (9oz) cherry tomatoes
6 tbsp fresh Pesto (see Cook's Tip, page 23)
25g (1oz) Parmesan shavings (see Cook's Tip, page 30)
salt
torn basil leaves to garnish

1. Cook the pasta in a large pan of lightly salted boiling water according to the pack instructions.

2. Meanwhile, gently toast the pinenuts in a dry frying pan, tossing them around until golden, then remove from the pan and set aside. Add the oil to the pan, followed by the garlic, mushrooms and courgettes. Add a splash of water to the pan, then cover and cook for 4–5 minutes.

3. Uncover the pan and add the tomatoes, then cook for a further 1–2 minutes.

4. Drain the pasta and return to the pan. Add the vegetables, pinenuts and pesto to the drained pasta. Toss well to combine and serve immediately, topped with the Parmesan shavings and garnished with basil.

Pasta Shells Stuffed with Spinach & Ricotta

Preparation Time 5 minutes • Cooking Time 30–35 minutes • Serves 6 • Per Serving 293 calories, 13g fat (of which 5g saturates), 33g carbohydrate, 0.8g salt • Vegetarian • Easy

450g (1lb) spinach, washed
125g (4oz) ricotta cheese (see Cook's Tips, page 177)
1 medium egg
a pinch of freshly grated nutmeg
grated zest of ½ lemon
50g (2oz) freshly grated Parmesan
225g (8oz) conchiglione pasta shells
½ quantity of Classic Tomato Sauce (see Cook's Tip)
25g (1oz) pinenuts
salt and ground black pepper

1. Put the spinach into a large pan, cover and cook over a low to medium heat for 2–3 minutes until wilted. Drain, squeeze out the excess liquid and chop finely.

2. Put the spinach into a large bowl with the ricotta and beat in the egg. Stir in the grated nutmeg, lemon zest and 25g (1oz) grated Parmesan, and season with salt and pepper.

3. Preheat the oven to 200°C (180°C fan oven) mark 6. Meanwhile, cook the pasta for 10 minutes or according to the pack instructions for oven-baked dishes. Drain well.

4. Spread the Classic Tomato Sauce in the base of an 18 × 23cm (7 × 9in) ovenproof dish. Fill the shells with spinach mixture and arrange on top of the sauce. Sprinkle with the remaining Parmesan and the pinenuts. Cook in the oven for 20–25 minutes until golden.

COOK'S TIP
Classic Tomato Sauce

Heat 1 tbsp olive oil in a largepan. Add 1 small onion, 1 grated carrot and 1 chopped celery stick, and fry gently for 20 minutes or until softened. Add 1 crushed garlic clove and ½ tbsp tomato purée, and fry for 1 minute. Stir in 2 × 400g cans plum tomatoes, then add 1 bay leaf, ½ tsp oregano and 2 tsp caster sugar. Simmer for 30 minutes or until thickened. Stir 3 tbsp freshly chopped basil into the sauce, then season with salt and ground black pepper. Serves 4.

Mixed Mushroom Cannelloni

Preparation Time 15 minutes • Cooking Time 50–55 minutes • Serves 4 • Per Serving 631 calories, 37g fat (of which 18g saturates), 50g carbohydrate, 1.9g salt • A Little Effort

6 sheets fresh lasagne
3 tbsp olive oil
1 small onion, finely sliced
3 garlic cloves, sliced
20g pack fresh thyme, finely chopped
225g (8oz) chestnut or brown-cap mushrooms, roughly chopped
125g (4oz) flat-cap mushrooms, roughly chopped
2 × 125g goat's cheese logs, with rind
350g carton cheese sauce
salt and ground black pepper
green salad to serve

1. Preheat the oven to 180°C (160°C fan oven) mark 4. Cook the lasagne in boiling water until just tender. Drain well and run it under cold water to cool. Keep covered with cold water until ready to use.

2. Heat the oil in a large pan and add the onion. Cook over a medium heat for 7–10 minutes until the onion is soft. Add the garlic and fry for 1–2 minutes. Keep a few slices of garlic to one side. Keep a little thyme for sprinkling later, then add the rest to the pan with the mushrooms. Cook for a further 5 minutes or until the mushrooms are golden brown and there is no excess liquid in the pan. Season, remove from the heat and put to one side.

3. Crumble one of the goat's cheese logs into the cooled mushroom mixture and stir together. Drain the lasagne sheets and pat dry with kitchen paper. Spoon 2–3 tbsp of the mushroom mixture along the long edge of each lasagne sheet, leaving a 1cm (½in) border. Roll up the pasta sheets and cut each roll in half. Put the pasta into a shallow ovenproof dish and spoon the cheese sauce over it. Slice the remaining goat's cheese into thick rounds and arrange across the middle of the pasta rolls. Sprinkle the reserved garlic and thyme on top. Cook in the oven for 30–35 minutes until golden and bubbling. Serve with a green salad.

COOK'S TIP
Fresh lasagne sheets wrapped around a filling are used here to make cannelloni, but you can also buy cannelloni tubes, which can easily be filled using a teaspoon.

Fast Macaroni Cheese

Preparation Time 5 minutes • Cooking Time 15 minutes • Serves 4 • Per Serving 1137 calories, 69g fat (of which 44g saturates), 96g carbohydrate, 2g salt • Easy

500g (1lb 2oz) macaroni
500ml (18fl oz) crème fraîche
200g (7oz) freshly grated Parmesan
2 tbsp ready-made English or Dijon mustard
5 tbsp freshly chopped flat-leafed parsley
salt and ground black pepper
green salad to serve

1. Cook the macaroni in a large pan of lightly salted boiling water according to the pack instructions. Drain and keep to one side.

2. Preheat the grill to high. Put the crème fraîche into a pan and heat gently. Stir in 175g (6oz) Parmesan, the mustard and parsley, and season well with black pepper. Stir the pasta into the sauce, spoon into bowls and sprinkle with the remaining cheese. Grill until golden and serve immediately with salad.

Very Easy Four-cheese Gnocchi

Preparation Time 3 minutes • Cooking Time 10 minutes • Serves 2 • Per Serving 630 calories, 28g fat
(of which 15g saturates), 77g carbohydrate, 1g salt • Vegetarian • Easy

350g pack fresh gnocchi
300g tub fresh four-cheese sauce
(see Cook's Tips, page 177)
240g pack sunblush tomatoes
2 tbsp freshly torn basil leaves,
plus basil sprigs to garnish
1 tbsp freshly grated Parmesan
(see Cook's Tips, page 177)
15g (½oz) butter, chopped
salt and ground black pepper
salad to serve

1. Cook the gnocchi in a large pan of lightly salted boiling water according to the pack instructions or until all the gnocchi have floated to the surface. Drain well and put the gnocchi back into the pan.

2. Preheat the grill. Add the four-cheese sauce and tomatoes to the gnocchi and heat gently, stirring, for 2 minutes.

3. Season with salt and pepper, then add the basil and stir again. Spoon into individual heatproof bowls, sprinkle a little Parmesan over each one and dot with butter.

4. Cook under the grill for 3–5 minutes until golden and bubbling. Garnish with basil sprigs and serve with salad.

Butternut Squash & Spinach Lasagne

Preparation Time 30 minutes • Cooking Time about 1 hour • Serves 6 • Per Serving 273 calories, 17g fat (of which 7g saturates), 18g carbohydrate, 0.6g salt • Vegetarian • Easy

1 butternut squash, peeled, halved, seeded and cut into 3cm (1¼in) cubes
2 tbsp olive oil
1 onion, sliced
25g (1oz) butter
25g (1oz) plain flour
600ml (1 pint) milk
250g (9oz) ricotta cheese (see Cook's Tips, page 177)
1 tsp freshly grated nutmeg
225g bag baby leaf spinach
6 'no need to pre-cook' lasagne sheets
50g (2oz) freshly grated pecorino cheese or Parmesan
salt and ground black pepper

1. Preheat the oven to 200°C (180°C fan oven) mark 6. Put the squash into a roasting tin with the oil, onion and 1 tbsp water. Mix well and season to taste with salt and pepper. Roast for 25 minutes, tossing halfway through.

2. To make the sauce melt the butter in a pan, then stir in the flour and cook over a medium heat for 1–2 minutes. Gradually add the milk, stirring constantly. Reduce the heat to a simmer and cook, stirring, for 5 minutes or until the sauce has thickened. Crumble the ricotta into the sauce and add the nutmeg.

Mix together thoroughly and season with salt and pepper.

3. Heat 1 tbsp water in a pan. Add the spinach, cover and cook until just wilted. Season generously.

4. Spoon the squash mixture into a 1.7 litre (3 pint) ovenproof dish. Layer the spinach on top, then cover with a third of the sauce, then the lasagne. Spoon the remaining sauce on top, season with salt and pepper and sprinkle with the grated cheese. Cook for 30–35 minutes until the cheese topping is golden and the pasta is cooked.

Artichoke & Mushroom Lasagne

Preparation Time 25 minutes • Cooking Time about 1½ hours • Serves 6 • Per Serving 322 calories, 21g fat (of which 11g saturates), 19g carbohydrate, 0.7g salt • Vegetarian • Easy

3 tbsp olive oil

225g (8oz) onions, roughly chopped

3 garlic cloves, crushed

25g (1oz) walnuts

1.1kg (2½lb) mixed mushrooms,
   such as brown-cap and button,
   roughly chopped

125g (4oz) cherry tomatoes

50g (2oz) butter, plus extra
   to grease

50g (2oz) plain flour

1.1 litres (2 pints) whole milk

2 bay leaves

2 tbsp lemon juice

200g pack fresh chilled lasagne

400g can artichoke hearts in water,
   drained and halved

75g (3oz) freshly grated Parmesan
   (see Cook's Tips, page 177)

salt and ground black pepper

fresh oregano sprigs to garnish
   (optional)

1. Heat the oil in a large pan and fry the onions gently for 10 minutes until soft. Add the garlic and walnuts, and fry for 3–4 minutes until pale golden. Stir in the chopped mushrooms and cook for 10 minutes. Let the mixture bubble briskly for a further 10 minutes or until all the liquid has evaporated. Add the tomatoes to the pan, then remove from the heat and set aside.

2. Preheat the oven to 200°C (180°C fan oven) mark 6. Melt the butter in a pan, add the flour and stir over a gentle heat for 1 minute. Slowly whisk in the milk until you have a smooth mixture. Bring to the boil, add the bay leaves, then stir over a gentle heat for 10 minutes until thickened and smooth. Add the lemon juice and season to taste with salt and pepper. Discard the bay leaves.

3. Grease a shallow ovenproof dish and layer lasagne sheets over the base. Spoon half the mushroom mixture over, then half the artichokes. Cover with a layer of lasagne and half the sauce. Spoon the remaining mushroom mixture over, then the remaining artichokes. Top with the remaining lasagne sheets. Stir the Parmesan into the remaining sauce and spoon evenly over the top of the lasagne.

4. Cook the lasagne in the oven for 40–50 minutes until golden and bubbling. Garnish with oregano sprigs if using, and serve.

GET AHEAD

To prepare ahead *Complete the recipe to the end of step 3, then cool, cover and chill for up to three hours.*
To use *Remove from the fridge about 30 minutes before cooking, then complete the recipe.*

Saffron Risotto with Lemon Chicken

Preparation Time 20 minutes • Cooking Time 30 minutes • Serves 4 • Per Serving 830 calories, 44g fat (of which 15g saturates), 50g carbohydrate, 0.9g salt • Easy

zest and juice of 1 lemon
a small handful of fresh parsley
25g (1oz) blanched almonds
1 tbsp dried thyme
1 garlic clove
75ml (2½fl oz) olive oil
450ml (¾ pint) hot chicken stock
4 boneless chicken breasts, skin on
50g (2oz) butter

225g (8oz) onions, finely chopped
a small pinch of saffron threads
225g (8oz) arborio rice
125ml (4fl oz) white wine
50g (2oz) freshly grated Parmesan
salt and ground black pepper
fresh thyme sprigs to garnish
lemon wedges to serve

1. Preheat the oven to 200°C (180°C fan oven) mark 6. Whiz the lemon zest, parsley, almonds, thyme and garlic in a food processor for a few seconds, then slowly add the oil and whiz until combined. Season with salt and pepper. Keep the hot stock at a gentle simmer.

2. Spread the lemon and herb mixture under the skin of the chicken. Put the chicken into a roasting tin, brush with 25g (1oz) melted butter and pour the lemon juice over it. Cook in the oven for 25 minutes, basting occasionally.

3. Heat the remaining butter in a pan. Add the onions and fry until soft. Stir in the saffron and rice. Add the wine to the rice. Add a ladleful of the hot stock to the rice and simmer, stirring, until absorbed. Continue adding the stock, a ladleful at a time until the rice is al dente (just tender but with a little bite at the centre) – this will take about 25 minutes. Take the pan off the heat and stir in the Parmesan. Serve with the chicken, pouring any juices from the roasting tin over it. Garnish with thyme sprigs and serve with lemon wedges.

Mushroom, Bacon & Leek Risotto

Preparation Time 10 minutes • Cooking Time about 30 minutes • Serves 4 • Per serving 452 calories, 13g fat
(of which 5g saturates), 62g carbohydrate, 2.6g salt • Easy

25g (1oz) dried mushrooms

**250g (9oz) dry-cure smoked bacon,
rind removed, chopped**

3 leeks, trimmed and chopped

300g (11oz) arborio rice

**25g (1oz) freshly grated Parmesan,
plus extra to serve**

**20g (¾oz) chives, chopped, plus
extra to garnish**

1. Put the mushrooms into a
large heatproof bowl and pour in
1.4 litres (2½ pints) boiling water.
Leave to soak for 10 minutes.

2. Meanwhile, fry the bacon and
leeks in a large pan – no need to
add oil – for 7–8 minutes until soft
and golden.

3. Stir in the rice and cook
for 1–2 minutes, then add the
mushrooms and their soaking
liquor. Cook at a gentle simmer,
stirring occasionally, for 15–20
minutes until the rice is cooked
and most of the liquid has been
absorbed.

4. Stir in the Parmesan and chives,
then sprinkle with extra Parmesan
and chives to serve.

COOK'S TIP
*To enrich the flavour, add a splash of
leftover dry sherry or white wine to
the pan when you add the rice.*

Prawn, Courgette & Leek Risotto

Preparation Time 10 minutes • Cooking Time 30 minutes • Serves 6 • Per Serving 320 calories, 7g fat
(of which 3g saturates), 49g carbohydrate, 1.3g salt • Easy

1 tbsp olive oil

25g (1oz) butter

1 leek, trimmed and finely
 chopped

2 courgettes, thinly sliced

2 garlic cloves, crushed

350g (12oz) arborio rice

1.6 litres (2¾ pints) hot vegetable
 stock

200g (7oz) cooked and peeled
 prawns

small bunch of parsley or mint,
 or a mixture of both, chopped

salt and ground black pepper

1. Heat the oil and half the butter in a large shallow pan. Add the leek, courgettes and garlic, and soften over a low heat. Add the rice and cook, stirring well, for 1 minute.

2. Meanwhile, put the hot stock into a pan and bring to the boil, then keep at a gentle simmer. Add a ladleful of the hot stock to the rice and simmer, stirring, until absorbed.

3. Continue adding the stock, a ladleful at a time until the rice is al dente (just tender but with a little bite at the centre) – this will take about 25 minutes and you may not need to add all the stock.

4. Add the prawns. Season to taste with salt and pepper, and stir in the remaining stock and the rest of the butter. Stir through and remove from the heat. Cover and leave to stand for a couple of minutes, then stir the chopped herbs through it. Serve immediately.

Smoked Haddock Risotto with Poached Eggs

Preparation Time 15 minutes • Cooking Time about 40 minutes • Serves 4 • Per Serving 508 calories, 17g fat (of which 8g saturates), 61g carbohydrate, 1.4g salt • Easy

200g (7oz) smoked haddock
50g (2oz) butter
1 large leek, white part only,
   trimmed and finely sliced
150ml (¼ pint) dry white wine
300g (11oz) arborio rice
1.1 litres (2 pints) hot chicken stock
4 large eggs
salt and ground black pepper
1 tbsp freshly chopped parsley
   to garnish

1. Put the haddock into a dish, pour boiling water over, cover and leave for 10 minutes. Flake the fish into bite-size pieces, discarding the skin and the bones.

2. Melt half the butter in a heavy-based pan. Add the leek and cook gently, stirring occasionally, for 15 minutes until softened. Add the wine and boil rapidly until it has almost evaporated. Add the rice and cook, for 1 minute, stirring to coat the grains.

3. Put the hot stock into a pan and bring to the boil, then keep at a gentle simmer. Add a ladleful of the hot stock to the rice. Simmer, stirring, until all the liquid has been absorbed. Continue adding the stock, a ladleful at a time until the rice is al dente (just tender but with a little bite at the centre) – this will take about 25 minutes and you may not need to add all the stock.

4. Meanwhile, bring a wide shallow pan of water to the boil. Crack an egg into a cup, turn off the heat under the pan and slip in the egg close to the water. Repeat with the other eggs and cover the pan. Leave to stand for 3 minutes.

5. Before adding the last ladleful of stock, stir in the pieces of fish and the remaining butter and check the seasoning. Heat the risotto through, adding the remaining stock if necessary. Remove the eggs with a slotted spoon and trim. Top each serving of risotto with a poached egg and a sprinkling of parsley.

MAIN COURSES

Slow-braised Garlic Chicken

Preparation Time 30 minutes • Cooking Time about 2 hours • Serves 6 • Per Serving 506 calories, 28g fat (of which 9g saturates), 10g carbohydrate, 1g salt • A Little Effort

2 tbsp olive oil
1 tbsp freshly chopped thyme
125g (4oz) chestnut mushrooms,
    finely chopped
6 whole chicken legs (drumsticks
    and thighs)
18 thin slices pancetta
2 tbsp plain flour
25g (1oz) butter
18 small shallots
12 garlic cloves, unpeeled but split
750ml bottle full-bodied white
    wine, such as Chardonnay
2 bay leaves
salt and ground black pepper

1. Preheat the oven to 180°C (160°C fan oven) mark 4. Heat 1 tbsp oil in a frying pan and fry the thyme and mushrooms until all the moisture has evaporated and the mixture is quite dry. Season and leave to cool.

2. Loosen the skin away from one chicken leg and spoon a little of the mushroom paste underneath. Season the leg all over with salt and pepper, then wrap three pancetta slices around the thigh end. Repeat with the remaining chicken legs, then dust using 1 tbsp flour.

3. Melt the butter in a frying pan with the remaining oil over a high heat. Fry the chicken legs, in batches of two, seam side down, until golden. Turn the legs, brown the other side, then transfer to a deep casserole. The browning process should take about 8–10 minutes per batch.

4. Put the shallots and garlic into the frying pan and cook for 10 minutes or until browned. Sprinkle the remaining flour over them and cook for 1 minute. Pour in the wine and bring to the boil, stirring. Pour into the casserole with the chicken and add the bay leaves. Cover and cook in the oven for 1½ hours. Serve hot.

GET AHEAD
To prepare ahead Complete the recipe to the end of step 4. Cool quickly, then freeze in an airtight container for up to one month.
To use Thaw overnight at cool room temperature. Preheat the oven to 220°C (200°C fan oven) mark 7. Put the chicken back into the casserole and reheat in the oven for 15 minutes. Reduce the oven temperature to 180°C (160°C fan oven) mark 4 and cook for a further 25 minutes.

Chicken in Red Wine

Preparation Time 15 minutes • Cooking Time 1 hour 10 minutes • Serves 4 • Per Serving 358 calories, 14g fat (of which 4g saturates), 8g carbohydrate, 1.1g salt • Easy

8 slices prosciutto
8 large boned and skinned chicken thighs
1 tbsp olive oil
1 fat garlic clove, crushed
about 12 shallots or button onions, peeled
225g (8oz) fresh shiitake mushrooms
1 tbsp plain flour
300ml (½ pint) red wine
300ml (½ pint) hot chicken stock
1 tbsp Worcestershire sauce
1 bay leaf
salt and ground black pepper
crusty bread to serve

1. Wrap a slice of prosciutto around each chicken thigh. Heat the olive oil in a large non-stick frying pan and fry the chicken pieces in batches for 8–10 minutes until golden all over. Transfer to a plate and put to one side.

2. Add the garlic and shallots or button onions and fry over a gentle heat for 5 minutes or until the shallots are beginning to soften and turn golden. Stir in the mushrooms and flour, and cook over a gentle heat for 1–2 minutes.

3. Put the chicken back into the pan and add the wine, hot stock, Worcestershire sauce and bay leaf. Season lightly with salt and pepper and bring to the boil. Boil for 5 minutes, then reduce the heat, cover the pan and simmer for 45 minutes or until the chicken is tender. Serve with crusty bread.

COOK'S TIPS
• *If you can't buy prosciutto, thinly cut smoked streaky bacon will work just as well.*
• *Use button mushrooms if you can't find shiitake.*

GET AHEAD
To prepare ahead Complete the recipe, cool quickly, then transfer to a freezerproof container and freeze for up to three months.
To use Thaw overnight at cool room temperature, then put back into a pan. Bring slowly to the boil, then simmer gently for 10–15 minutes until piping hot.

Caribbean Chicken

Preparation Time 40 minutes, plus at least 4 hours marinating • Cooking Time 45–50 minutes • Serves 5 •
Per Serving 617 calories, 39g fat (of which 12g saturates), 25g carbohydrate, 2.1g salt • Easy

10 skinless chicken pieces,
   scored with a knife
1 tbsp each ground coriander
   and paprika
2 tsp ground cumin
a pinch of freshly grated nutmeg
1 fresh Scotch bonnet or other hot
   red chilli, seeded and chopped
   (see Cook's Tip, page 20)
1 onion, chopped
5 fresh thyme sprigs, leaves
   stripped, plus extra to garnish
4 garlic cloves, crushed
2 tbsp dark soy sauce
juice of 1 lemon

2 tbsp vegetable oil
2 tbsp light muscovado sugar
350g (12oz) American easy-cook
   rice
25g (1oz) butter
2 × 300g cans black-eyed beans,
   drained and rinsed
salt and ground black pepper

1. Put the chicken into a bowl and sprinkle with ½ tsp salt, some pepper, the coriander, paprika, cumin and nutmeg. Add the chilli, onion, thyme leaves and garlic, then pour the soy sauce and lemon juice over and stir to combine. Cover and chill for at least 4 hours.

2. Heat a 3.4 litre (6 pint) heavy-based pan over a medium heat for 2 minutes. Add the oil and sugar and cook for 3 minutes to a rich caramel colour – don't let it burn. Remove the chicken from the marinade and add to the caramel mixture. Cover and cook over a medium heat for 5 minutes. Turn the chicken and cook, covered, for 5 minutes or until evenly browned. Add the onion, chilli and any juices from the marinade. Turn again, then cover and cook for 10 minutes. Stir in the rice and add 900ml (1½ pints) water. Add the butter and ½ tsp salt. Cover and simmer for 20 minutes or until the rice is tender and most of the liquid has been absorbed.

3. Mix in the beans, cover and cook for 3–5 minutes until the liquid has been absorbed, taking care that the rice doesn't stick to the bottom of the pan. Garnish with thyme and serve hot.

Chicken Cacciatore

Preparation Time 5 minutes • Cooking Time 40 minutes • Serves 4 • Per Serving 327 calories, 17g fat (of which 4g saturates), 3g carbohydrate, 1.3g salt • Easy

2 tbsp olive oil
8 boneless, skinless chicken thighs
2 garlic cloves, crushed
1 tsp dried thyme
1 tsp dried tarragon
150ml (¼ pint) white wine
400g can chopped tomatoes
12 pitted black olives
12 capers, rinsed and drained
ground black pepper
brown rice and broad beans or peas
    to serve

1. Heat the oil in a flameproof casserole over a high heat. Add the chicken and brown all over. Reduce the heat and add the garlic, thyme, tarragon and wine to the casserole. Stir for 1 minute, then add the tomatoes and season with pepper.

2. Bring to the boil, then reduce the heat, cover the casserole and simmer for 20 minutes or until the chicken is tender.

3. Lift the chicken out of the casserole and put to one side. Bubble the sauce for 5 minutes or until thickened, add the olives and capers, stir well and cook for a further 2–3 minutes.

4. Put the chicken into the sauce. Serve with brown rice and broad beans or peas.

Oven-baked Chicken with Garlic Potatoes

Preparation Time 10 minutes • Cooking Time 1½ hours • Serves 6 • Per Serving 376 calories, 16g fat (of which 5g saturates), 32g carbohydrate, 1.2g salt • Easy

2 medium baking potatoes, thinly sliced

a little freshly grated nutmeg

600ml (1 pint) white sauce (use a ready-made sauce or make your own, see Cook's Tip)

½ × 390g can fried onions

250g (9oz) frozen peas

450g (1lb) cooked chicken, shredded

20g pack garlic butter, sliced

a little butter to grease

salt and ground black pepper

steamed vegetables and Granary bread (optional) to serve

1. Preheat the oven to 180°C (160°C fan oven) mark 4. Layer half the potatoes over the base of a 2.4 litre (4¼ pint) shallow ovenproof dish and season with the nutmeg, salt and pepper. Pour the white sauce over and shake the dish, so that the sauce settles through the gaps in the potatoes.

2. Spread half the onions on top, then scatter with half the peas. Arrange the shredded chicken on top, then add the remaining peas and onions. Finish with the remaining potato, arranged in an even layer, and dot with garlic butter. Season with salt and pepper.

3. Cover tightly with buttered foil and cook for 1 hour. Increase the heat to 200°C (180°C fan oven) mark 6, remove the foil and continue to cook for 20–30 minutes until the potatoes are golden and tender. Serve with steamed vegetables and, if you like, some Granary bread to mop up the juices.

COOK'S TIP

White Sauce

To make 600ml (1 pint) white sauce, melt 25g (1oz) butter in a pan, then stir in 25g (1oz) plain flour. Cook, stirring constantly, for 1 minute. Remove from the heat and gradually pour in 600ml (1 pint) milk, beating after each addition. Return to the heat and cook, stirring, until the sauce has thickened and is velvety and smooth. Season with salt, black pepper and freshly grated nutmeg.

One-pan Chicken with Tomatoes

Preparation Time 5 minutes • Cooking Time 20–25 minutes • Serves 4 • Per Serving 238 calories, 4g fat
(of which 1g saturates), 20g carbohydrate, 1g salt • Easy

4 chicken thighs
1 red onion, sliced
400g can chopped tomatoes
  with herbs
400g can mixed beans, drained
  and rinsed
2 tsp balsamic vinegar
salt and ground black pepper
freshly chopped flat-leafed parsley
  to garnish

1. Heat a non-stick pan and fry
the chicken thighs, skin side down,
until golden. Turn over and fry for
5 minutes.

2. Add the onion and fry for
5 minutes. Add the tomatoes,
mixed beans and vinegar, cover
the pan and simmer for 10–12
minutes until piping hot. Check the
seasoning. Garnish with parsley
and serve immediately.

**TRY SOMETHING
DIFFERENT**
*Use flageolet beans or other canned
beans instead of mixed beans, and
garnish with fresh basil or oregano.*

Coq au Vin

Preparation Time 45 minutes • Cooking Time about 1 hour • Serves 4 • Per Serving 787 calories, 51g fat (of which 22g saturates), 24g carbohydrate, 1.5g salt • A Little Effort

750ml bottle full-bodied white wine, such as Chardonnay

4 tbsp brandy

2 bouquet garni (see Cook's Tip, page 22)

1 garlic clove, bruised

flour to coat

1 chicken, about 1.4kg (3lb), jointed, or 2 boneless breasts, halved, plus 2 drumsticks and 2 thighs

125g (4oz) butter

125g (4oz) rindless unsmoked bacon rashers, cut into strips

225g (8oz) baby onions, peeled with root ends intact

225g (8oz) brown-cap mushrooms, halved, or quartered if large

25g (1oz) butter mixed with 25g (1oz) plain flour (beurre manié)

salt and ground black pepper

buttered noodles or rice to serve

1. Preheat the oven to 180°C (160°C fan oven) mark 4. Pour the wine and brandy into a pan. Add 1 bouquet garni and the garlic. Bring to the boil, then reduce the heat and simmer until reduced by half. Cool.

2. Season the flour with salt and pepper and use to coat the chicken joints lightly. Melt half the butter in a large frying pan. When foaming, add the chicken joints and brown all over (in batches if necessary). Transfer to a flameproof casserole. Add the bacon to the frying pan and fry until golden. Remove with a slotted spoon and add to the chicken.

3. Strain the cooled reduced wine mixture over the chicken and add the other bouquet garni. Bring to the boil, cover and cook in the oven for 30 minutes.

4. Meanwhile, melt the remaining butter in a frying pan and fry the onions until tender and lightly browned. Add the mushrooms and fry until softened. Add the mushrooms and onions to the casserole, cover and cook for a further 10 minutes or until the chicken is tender.

5. Lift out the chicken and vegetables with a slotted spoon and put into a warmed serving dish. Cover and keep warm.

6. Bring the cooking liquid in the casserole to the boil on the hob. Whisk in the beurre manié, a piece at a time, until the sauce is shiny and syrupy. Check the seasoning.

7. Pour the sauce over the chicken. Serve with buttered noodles or rice.

Chicken Tagine with Apricots & Almonds

Preparation Time 10 minutes • Cooking Time about 1 hour • Serves 4 • Per Serving 376 calories, 22g fat (of which 4g saturates), 19g carbohydrate, 0.5g salt • Easy

2 tbsp olive oil
4 chicken thighs
1 onion, chopped
2 tsp ground cinnamon
2 tbsp clear honey
150g (5oz) ready-to-eat dried apricots
75g (3oz) blanched almonds
250ml (9fl oz) hot chicken stock
salt and ground black pepper
flaked almonds to garnish
couscous to serve

1. Heat 1 tbsp olive oil in a large flameproof casserole over a medium heat. Add the chicken and fry for 5 minutes or until brown. Remove from the casserole and put to one side to keep warm.

2. Add the onion to the casserole with the remaining oil and fry for 10 minutes or until softened.

3. Put the chicken back into the casserole with the cinnamon, honey, apricots, almonds and hot stock. Season well with salt and pepper, stir once, then cover and bring to the boil. Reduce the heat and simmer for 45 minutes or until the chicken is falling off the bone

4. Garnish with the flaked almonds and serve hot with couscous.

Chicken Rarebit

Preparation Time 5 minutes • Cooking Time 25 minutes • Serves 4 • Per Serving 446 calories, 24g fat (of which 14g saturates), 9g carbohydrate, 1.3g salt • Easy

4 large chicken breasts, with skin, about 150g (5oz) each
15g (½oz) butter
1 tbsp plain flour
75ml (2½fl oz) full-fat milk
175g (6oz) Gruyère cheese, grated
25g (1oz) fresh white breadcrumbs
1 tsp ready-made English mustard
2 fat garlic cloves, crushed
1 medium egg yolk
boiled new potatoes and green beans to serve

1. Preheat the oven to 200°C (180°C fan oven) mark 6. Put the chicken in a single layer into an ovenproof dish and roast for 20 minutes or until cooked through.

2. Meanwhile, melt the butter in a pan over a low heat, then add the flour and stir for 1 minute. Gradually add the milk and stir to make a smooth sauce.

3. Add the cheese, breadcrumbs, mustard and garlic to the sauce and cook for 1 minute. Cool briefly, then beat in the egg yolk. Preheat the grill to medium-high.

4. Discard the skin from the cooked chicken and beat any juices from the dish into the cheese mixture. Spread the paste evenly over each chicken breast, then grill for 2–3 minutes until golden. Serve with boiled new potatoes and green beans.

One-pot Chicken

Preparation Time 20 minutes • Cooking Time 1 hour 40 minutes • Serves 6 • Per Serving 474 calories, 33g fat (of which 9g saturates), 6g carbohydrate, 0.6g salt • Easy

2 tbsp olive oil
1 large onion, cut into wedges
2 rindless streaky bacon rashers, chopped
1 chicken, about 1.6kg (3½lb)
6 carrots
2 small turnips, cut into wedges
1 garlic clove, crushed
1 bouquet garni (see Cook's Tip, page 22)
600ml (1 pint) hot chicken stock
100ml (3½fl oz) dry white wine
12 button mushrooms
3 tbsp freshly chopped flat-leafed parsley
salt and ground black pepper
mashed potatoes to serve

1. Heat the olive oil in a non-stick flameproof casserole, then add the onion and bacon and fry for 5 minutes or until golden. Remove from the pan and put aside.

2. Add the whole chicken to the casserole and fry for 10 minutes, turning carefully to brown all over. Remove and set aside.

3. Preheat the oven to 200°C (180°C fan oven) mark 6. Add the carrots, turnips and garlic to the casserole. Fry for 5 minutes, then add the bacon and onion. Put the chicken back into the casserole. Add the bouquet garni, hot stock and wine, and season with salt and pepper. Bring to a simmer, then cover and cook in the oven for 30 minutes.

4. Remove the casserole from the oven and add the mushrooms.

Baste the chicken, then re-cover and cook for a further 50 minutes.

5. Lift out the chicken, then stir the parsley into the cooking liquid. Carve the chicken and serve with the vegetables, cooking liquid and mashed potatoes.

TRY SOMETHING DIFFERENT
Use chicken pieces such as drumsticks or thighs, reducing the cooking time in step 4 to 20 minutes.

Peppered Winter Stew

Preparation Time 20 minutes • Cooking Time 2¾ hours • Serves 6 • Per Serving 540 calories, 24g fat (of which 7g saturates), 24g carbohydrate, 1.5g salt • Easy

25g (1oz) plain flour

900g (2lb) stewing venison, beef or lamb, cut into 4cm (1½in) cubes

5 tbsp oil

225g (8oz) button onions or shallots, peeled with root end intact

225g (8oz) onion, finely chopped

4 garlic cloves, crushed

2 tbsp tomato purée

125ml (4fl oz) red wine vinegar

750ml bottle red wine

2 tbsp redcurrant jelly

1 small bunch of fresh thyme, plus extra sprigs to garnish (optional)

4 bay leaves

6 cloves

900g (2lb) mixed root vegetables, such as carrots, parsnips, turnips and celeriac, cut into 4cm (1½in) chunks; carrots cut a little smaller

600–900ml (1–1½ pints) beef stock

salt and ground black pepper

1. Preheat the oven to 180°C (160°C fan oven) mark 4. Put the flour into a plastic bag, season with salt and pepper, then toss the meat in it.

2. Heat 3 tbsp oil in a large flameproof casserole over a medium heat and brown the meat well in small batches. Remove and put to one side.

3. Heat the remaining oil and fry the button onions or shallots for 5 minutes or until golden. Add the chopped onion and the garlic and cook, stirring, until soft and golden. Add the tomato purée and cook for a further 2 minutes, then add the vinegar and wine and bring to the boil. Bubble for 10 minutes.

4. Add the redcurrant jelly, thyme, bay leaves, 1 tbsp coarsely ground black pepper, the cloves and meat to the pan, with the vegetables and enough stock to barely cover the meat and vegetables. Bring to the boil, then reduce the heat, cover the pan and cook in the oven for 1¾–2¼ hours until the meat is very tender. Serve hot, garnished with thyme sprigs, if you like.

FREEZING TIP

To freeze *Complete the recipe to the end of step 4, without the garnish. Cool quickly and put in a freezerproof container. Seal and freeze for up to one month.*

To use *Thaw overnight at cool room temperature. Preheat the oven to 180°C (160°C fan oven) mark 4. Put into a flameproof casserole and add an extra 150ml (¼ pint) beef stock. Bring to the boil. Cover and reheat for 30 minutes.*

Ribs & Beans in a Sticky Barbecue Sauce

Preparation time 10 minutes • Cooking time 1¼ hours • Serves 4 • Per serving 620 calories, 25g fat (of which 10g saturates), 53g carbohydrate, 1g salt

8 meaty pork spare ribs
1 large onion, chopped
2 large garlic cloves, chopped
4 tbsp light muscovado sugar
1 tbsp French mustard
4 tbsp sun-dried tomato paste
150g (5oz) passata
4 tbsp malt vinegar
4 tbsp tomato ketchup
2 tbsp Worcestershire sauce
568ml can dry cider
2 × 410g cans black-eye beans,
    drained and rinsed
4 tbsp freshly chopped parsley
salt and ground black pepper

1. Trim the spare ribs of excess fat if necessary and season with salt and pepper.

2. Put the onion, garlic, sugar, mustard, tomato paste, passata, vinegar, ketchup and Worcestershire sauce into a large roasting tin and stir well. Add the spare ribs and stir to coat in the sauce.

3. Cook in the oven at 210°C (190°C fan oven) mark 6½ for 30 minutes, then turn the ribs over and cook for a further 30 minutes until they are crisp and brown.

4. Add the cider and stir to mix well with the sauce, scraping up the sediment from the bottom of the pan. Add the black-eye beans, stir and return to the oven for a further 15 minutes. Scatter with the chopped parsley to serve.

TRY SOMETHING DIFFERENT
Use canned haricot or pinto beans instead of black-eye beans.

Spanish-style Pork

Preparation Time 15 minutes • Cooking Time 25 minutes • Per Serving 349 calories, 12g fat (of which 3g saturates), 26g carbohydrate, 1.2g salt • Serves 4 • Easy

500g (1lb 2oz) pork fillet, trimmed and sliced
2 tbsp olive oil
1 Spanish onion, chopped
2 celery sticks, finely chopped
2 tsp smoked paprika
1 tbsp tomato purée
750ml (1¼ pints) hot chicken stock
400g can butter beans, drained and rinsed
¼ Savoy cabbage, finely shredded
200g (7oz) green beans, trimmed and halved
salt and ground black pepper
1 tbsp freshly chopped rosemary to garnish
lemon wedges and crusty bread to serve

1. Lay the pork out on a board, cover with clingfilm and flatten slightly with a rolling pin. Heat 1 tbsp oil in a frying pan and fry the pork over a medium to high heat until browned. Remove from the pan and set aside.

2. Heat the remaining oil and gently fry the chopped onion and celery for 10 minutes or until softened. Stir in the paprika and tomato purée and cook for 1 minute. Stir in the hot stock, butter beans and cabbage. Season with salt and pepper.

3. Return the pork to the pan and bring to the boil, then reduce the heat and simmer for 10 minutes, adding the green beans for the last 4 minutes. Garnish with rosemary and serve with lemon wedges and crusty bread on the side.

Italian Sausage Stew

Preparation Time 10 minutes, plus soaking • Cooking Time 15 minutes • Serves 4 • Per Serving 443 calories, 35g fat (of which 12g saturates), 6g carbohydrate, 3.4g salt • Easy

25g (1oz) dried porcini mushrooms
2 tbsp olive oil
1 onion, sliced
2 garlic cloves, chopped
1 small red chilli, seeded and finely chopped (see Cook's Tip, page 20)
2 fresh rosemary stalks, leaves picked
300g (11oz) whole rustic Italian salami sausages, such as salami Milano, cut into 1cm (½in) slices
400g can chopped tomatoes

200ml (7fl oz) red wine
1 tsp salt
175g (6oz) quick-cook or instant polenta
50g (2oz) butter
50g (2oz) freshly grated Parmesan, plus extra shavings to serve (optional) (see Cook's Tip, page 30)
75g (3oz) Fontina cheese, cubed
ground black pepper
green or mixed salad to serve

1. Put the mushrooms into a small bowl, pour 100ml (3½fl oz) boiling water over them and leave to soak for 20 minutes, or soften in the microwave on full power for 3½ minutes. Set aside to cool.

2. Heat the oil in a large frying pan over a low heat, add the onion, garlic and chilli, and cook gently for 5 minutes. Add half the rosemary leaves to the pan, stirring.

3. Add the salami and fry for 2 minutes on each side or until browned. Drain and chop the soaked mushrooms and add to the pan. Add the tomatoes and wine, then season with pepper. Simmer, uncovered, for 5 minutes.

4. Put 750ml (1¼ pints) boiling water and the salt into a pan. Bring back to the boil, add the polenta and cook according to the pack instructions. Add the butter and both cheeses and mix together well.

5. To serve, divide the polenta among four plates and top with the Parmesan shavings, if you like. Spoon some sausage stew alongside each serving of polenta and garnish with the remaining rosemary. Serve immediately with a green or mixed side salad.

One-pot Gammon Stew

Preparation Time 15 minutes • Cooking Time 1 hour 10 minutes • Serves 4 • Per Serving 680 calories, 30g fat (of which 11g saturates), 41g carbohydrate, 6.3g salt • Easy

1 tbsp olive oil

1.1kg (2½lb) smoked gammon joint

8 shallots, blanched in boiling water, drained, peeled and chopped into chunks

3 carrots, chopped into chunks

3 celery sticks, chopped into chunks

4 large Desiree potatoes, unpeeled

450ml (¾ pint) each apple juice and hot vegetable stock

½ small Savoy cabbage

25g (1oz) butter

1. Preheat the oven to 190°C (170°C fan oven) mark 5. Heat the oil in a large flameproof casserole. Add the gammon and cook for 5 minutes or until brown all over. Remove from the pan.

2. Add the shallots, carrots and celery to the pan and fry for 3–4 minutes until starting to soften.

3. Return the gammon to the pan. Chop the potatoes into quarters and add to the pan with the apple juice and hot stock. Cover and bring to the boil, then transfer to the oven and cook for 50 minutes or until the meat is cooked through and the vegetables are tender.

4. Remove from the oven and put the dish back on the hob over a low heat. Shred the cabbage and stir into the pan. Simmer for 2–3 minutes, then stir in the butter and serve.

Pork & Apple Hotpot

Preparation Time 15 minutes • Cooking Time 2–2¼ hours • Serves 4 • Per Serving 592 calories, 18g fat
(of which 7g saturates), 56g carbohydrate, 1g salt • Easy

1 tbsp olive oil
900g (2lb) pork shoulder steaks
3 onions, cut into wedges
1 large Bramley apple, peeled,
    cored and thickly sliced
1 tbsp plain flour
600ml (1 pint) hot, weak chicken
    or vegetable stock
¼ Savoy cabbage, sliced
2 fresh thyme sprigs
900g (2lb) large potatoes, cut
    into 2cm (¾in) slices
25g (1oz) butter
salt and ground black pepper

1. Preheat the oven to 170°C (150°C fan oven) mark 3. In a large non-stick flameproof casserole, heat the oil until very hot, then fry the steaks, two at a time, for 5 minutes or until golden all over. Remove the steaks from the pan and put aside.

2. In the same casserole, fry the onions for 10 minutes or until soft – add a little water if they start to stick. Stir in the apple and cook for 1 minute, then add the flour to soak up the juices. Gradually add the hot stock and stir until smooth. Season. Stir in the cabbage and add the pork.

3. Throw in the thyme, overlap the potato slices on top, then dot with the butter. Cover with a tight-fitting lid and cook near the top of the oven for 1 hour. Remove the lid and cook for 30–45 minutes until the potatoes are tender and golden.

COOK'S TIP
Put the hotpot under the grill for 2–3 minutes to crisp up the potatoes, if you like.

FREEZING TIP
If you are going to freeze this dish, use a freezerproof casserole.
To freeze *Complete the recipe, cool quickly, then freeze in the casserole for up to three months.*
To use *Thaw overnight at cool room temperature. Preheat the oven to 180°C (160°C fan oven) mark 4. Pour 50ml (2fl oz) hot stock over the hotpot, then cover and reheat for 30 minutes or until piping hot. Uncover and crisp the potatoes under the grill for 2–3 minutes.*

Warming Winter Casserole

Preparation Time 20 minutes • Cooking Time 1 hour • Serves 4 • Per Serving 407 calories, 16g fat (of which 3g saturates), 32g carbohydrate, 1g salt • Easy

2 tbsp olive oil

500g (1lb 2oz) pork fillet, cut into cubes

1 onion, finely chopped

2 garlic cloves, finely chopped

1 tsp ground cinnamon

1 tbsp ground coriander

1 tsp ground cumin

2.5cm (1in) piece fresh root ginger, peeled and grated

400g can mixed beans or chickpeas, drained

1 red pepper, seeded and sliced

50g (2oz) ready-to-eat dried apricots, roughly chopped

300ml (½ pint) chicken stock

25g (1oz) flaked almonds, toasted

salt and ground black pepper

freshly chopped flat-leafed parsley to garnish

brown basmati rice to serve

1. Heat 1 tbsp oil in a flameproof casserole, add the pork and fry, in batches, until brown all over. Remove and put to one side. Add the remaining oil, then add the onion and cook for 10 minutes or until softened. Return the pork to the casserole, add the garlic, spices and ginger, and cook for 2 minutes.

2. Add the mixed beans, red pepper, apricots and stock. Season well with salt and pepper, then stir and bring to the boil. Reduce the heat to the lowest setting, cover the pan and simmer for 40 minutes, adding a little extra stock if it begins to looks dry.

3. Sprinkle with the almonds and parsley, check the seasoning and serve with brown basmati rice.

TRY SOMETHING DIFFERENT
Instead of pork, use the same quantity of lean lamb, such as leg, trimmed of excess fat and cut into cubes.

Belly of Pork with Cider & Rosemary

Preparation Time 30 minutes, plus cooling and chilling • Cooking Time about 4½ hours • Serves 8 •
Per Serving 694 calories, 52g fat (of which 19g saturates), 9g carbohydrate, 0.5g salt • Easy

2kg (4½lb) piece pork belly roast,
   on the bone
500ml bottle medium cider
600ml (1 pint) hot chicken stock
6–8 fresh rosemary sprigs
3 fat garlic cloves, halved
2 tbsp olive oil
grated zest and juice of 1 large
   orange and 1 lemon
3 tbsp light muscovado sugar
25g (1oz) softened butter, mixed
   with 1 tbsp plain flour
salt and ground black pepper
mixed vegetables to serve

1. Preheat the oven to 150°C (130°C fan oven) mark 2. Put the pork, skin side up, in a roasting tin just large enough to hold it. Add the cider, hot stock and half the rosemary. Bring to the boil on the hob, then cover with foil and cook in the oven for 4 hours. Leave to cool in the cooking liquid.

2. Strip the leaves from the remaining rosemary and chop. Put into a mortar with the garlic, oil, orange and lemon zest, 1 tsp salt and 1 tbsp sugar. Pound with a pestle for 3–4 minutes to make a rough paste.

3. Remove the pork from the tin (keep the cooking liquid) and slice off the rind from the top layer of fat. Put to one side. Score the fat into a diamond pattern and rub in the rosemary paste. Cover loosely with clingfilm and chill until required.

4. Pat the rind dry with kitchen paper and put it (fat side up) on a foil-lined baking sheet. Cook under a hot grill, about 10cm (4in) away from the heat, for 5 minutes. Turn over, sprinkle lightly with salt, then grill for 7–10 minutes until crisp. Cool, then cut the crackling into rough pieces.

5. Make the gravy. Strain the cooking liquid into a pan. Add the orange and lemon juice and the remaining 2 tbsp sugar, bring to the boil and bubble until reduced by half. Whisk the butter mixture into the liquid and boil for 4–5 minutes until thickened. Put to one side.

6. When almost ready to serve, preheat the oven to 220°C (200°C fan oven) mark 7. Cook the pork, uncovered, in a roasting tin for 20 minutes or until piping hot. Wrap the crackling in foil and warm in the oven for the last 5 minutes of the cooking time. Heat the gravy on the hob. Carve the pork into slices and serve with the crackling, gravy and vegetables.

Lamb Chops with Crispy Garlic Potatoes

Preparation Time 10 minutes • Cooking Time 20 minutes • Serves 4 • Per Serving 835 calories, 45g fat (of which 19g saturates), 22g carbohydrate, 0.7g salt • Easy

2 tbsp Mint Sauce (see Cook's Tips)
8 small lamb chops
3 medium potatoes, cut into 5mm (¼in) slices
2 tbsp Garlic-infused Olive Oil (see Cook's Tips)
1 tbsp olive oil
salt and ground black pepper
steamed green beans to serve

1. Spread the mint sauce over the lamb chops and leave to marinate while you prepare the potatoes.

2. Boil the potatoes in a pan of lightly salted water for 2 minutes or until just starting to soften. Drain, tip back into the pan and season with salt and pepper, then add the garlic oil and toss to combine.

3. Meanwhile, heat the olive oil in a large frying pan and fry the chops for 4–5 minutes on each side until just cooked, adding a splash of boiling water to the pan to make a sauce. Remove the chops and sauce from the pan and keep warm.

4. Add the potatoes to the pan. Fry over a medium heat for 10–12 minutes until crisp and golden. Divide the potatoes, chops and sauce among four warmed plates and serve with green beans.

COOK'S TIPS

Mint Sauce
Finely chop 20g (¾oz) fresh mint and mix with 1 tbsp each olive oil and white wine vinegar.

Garlic-infused Olive Oil
Gently heat 2 tbsp olive oil with peeled sliced garlic for 5 minutes and use immediately. Do not store.

Braised Lamb Shanks

Preparation Time 20–25 minutes • Cooking Time 2¾ hours • Serves 6 • Per Serving 355 calories, 16g fat
(of which 6g saturates), 23g carbohydrate, 1.2g salt • Easy

6 small lamb shanks
**450g (1lb) shallots, peeled but
  left whole**
**2 medium aubergines, cut into
  small dice**
2 tbsp olive oil
3 tbsp harissa paste
**pared zest of 1 orange and juice
  of 3 large oranges**
200ml (7fl oz) medium sherry
700g (1½lb) passata
**300ml (½ pint) hot vegetable or
  lamb stock**
**75g (3oz) ready-to-eat dried
  apricots**
75g (3oz) cherries (optional)
a large pinch of saffron
**couscous and French beans
  (optional) to serve**

1. Preheat the oven to 170°C
(150°C fan oven) mark 3. Heat a
large flameproof casserole over
a medium heat and brown the
lamb shanks all over. Allow 10–12
minutes to do this. The flavour and
colour of the finished dish depend
on the meat taking on a good
deep colour now.

2. Remove the lamb and put to one
side. Add the shallots, aubergines
and oil to the casserole and cook
over a high heat, stirring from
time to time, until the shallots
and aubergines are golden and
beginning to soften.

3. Reduce the heat and add the
lamb and all the other ingredients
except the couscous and beans.
The liquid should come halfway up
the shanks. Bring to the boil, then
cover tightly and cook in the oven
for 2½ hours. Test the lamb with a
fork – it should be so tender that it
almost falls off the bone.

4. If the cooking liquid looks too
thin, remove the lamb to a heated
serving plate, then bubble the
sauce on the hob until reduced
and thickened. Put the lamb back
into the casserole. Serve with
couscous and French beans, if
you like.

COOK'S TIP
*Cooking lamb shanks in a rich
sauce in the oven at a low
temperature makes the meat
meltingly tender.*

Greek Lamb & Feta Layer

Preparation Time 20 minutes • Cooking Time about 1 hour 50 minutes • Serves 8 • Per Serving 684 calories, 45g fat (of which 20g saturates), 32g carbohydrate, 1.8g salt • A Little Effort

5 tbsp olive oil
1 large onion, finely chopped
900g (2lb) minced lamb
2 garlic cloves, crushed
2 tbsp tomato purée
2 × 400g cans plum tomatoes in tomato juice
3 tbsp Worcestershire sauce
2 tbsp freshly chopped oregano
3 large potatoes, about 1kg (2¼lb) total weight, unpeeled
2 large aubergines, trimmed and cut into 5mm (¼in) slices
1kg (2¼lb) Greek yogurt
4 large eggs
50g (2oz) freshly grated Parmesan

a pinch of freshly grated nutmeg
200g (7oz) feta cheese, crumbled
salt and ground black pepper

1. Heat 2 tbsp oil in a large pan, add the onion and cook over a low heat for 10 minutes or until soft. Put the mince into a large non-stick frying pan and cook over a high heat, breaking it up with a spoon, until no liquid remains and the lamb is brown, 10–15 minutes. Add the garlic and tomato purée and cook for 2 minutes. Add the lamb to the onion with the tomatoes,

Worcestershire sauce and oregano. Bring to the boil and season. Simmer for 30–40 minutes until the lamb is tender.

2. Meanwhile, cook the potatoes in lightly salted boiling water for 20–30 minutes until tender, then drain and cool. Peel and slice thickly. Preheat the oven to 180°C (160°C fan oven) mark 4. Brush the aubergine slices with the remaining oil. Preheat two non-stick frying pans and cook the aubergine slices for 2–3 minutes on each side until soft. Mix together the yogurt, eggs and half the Parmesan, season the sauce to taste with salt and pepper, then add the nutmeg.

3. Divide the lamb between two 1.4 litre (2½ pint) ovenproof dishes or eight individual dishes. Layer the potato, feta and aubergine on top. Pour the yogurt sauce over and sprinkle with the remaining Parmesan. Cook for 35–40 minutes until the top has browned and it's piping hot in the centre.

FREEZING TIP

To freeze When you have layered the lamb, vegetables, feta, yogurt sauce and Parmesan in the dishes at step 3, cool, wrap and freeze for up to three months.
To use Thaw overnight at cool room temperature. Cook at 190°C (170°C fan oven) mark 5 for 45–50 minutes until piping hot in the centre.

Irish Stew

Preparation Time 15 minutes • Cooking Time 2 hours • Serves 4 • Per Serving 419 calories, 20g fat (of which 9g saturates), 24g carbohydrate, 0.6g salt • Easy

700g (1½lb) middle neck lamb cutlets, fat trimmed
2 onions, thinly sliced
450g (1lb) potatoes, thinly sliced
1 tbsp freshly chopped parsley, plus extra to garnish
1 tbsp dried thyme
300ml (½ pint) lamb stock
salt and ground black pepper

1. Preheat the oven to 170°C (150°C fan oven) mark 3. Layer the meat, onions and potatoes in a deep casserole, sprinkling some herbs and seasoning between each layer. Finish with a layer of potato, overlapping the slices neatly.

2. Pour the stock over the potatoes, then cover with greaseproof paper and a lid. Cook in the oven for 2 hours or until the meat is tender.

3. Preheat the grill. Take the lid off the casserole and remove the paper. Put under the grill and brown the top. Sprinkle with parsley and serve the stew immediately.

Italian Lamb Stew

Preparation Time 35 minutes • Cooking Time 3¾ hours • Serves 6 • Per Serving 824 calories, 41g fat
(of which 12g saturates), 25g carbohydrate, 1.8g salt • Easy

2 half legs of lamb (knuckle ends)
2 tbsp olive oil
75g (3oz) butter
275g (10oz) onions, finely chopped
175g (6oz) carrots, finely chopped
175g (6oz) celery, finely chopped
2 tbsp dried porcini pieces (see
   Cook's Tip) or 125g (4oz) brown-
   cap mushrooms, finely chopped
9 pieces sun-dried tomato, finely
   chopped
150g (5oz) Italian-style spicy
   sausage or salami, thickly sliced
600ml (1 pint) red wine

400g (14oz) passata
600ml (1 pint) vegetable stock
125g (4oz) pasta shapes
15g (½oz) freshly grated Parmesan
freshly chopped flat-leafed parsley
   to garnish

1. Preheat the oven to 240°C (220°C fan oven) mark 9. Put the lamb in a large roasting tin and drizzle 1 tbsp oil over it. Roast for 35 minutes.

2. Meanwhile, melt the butter with the remaining oil in a large flameproof casserole. Stir in the onions, carrots and celery and cook, stirring, for 10–15 minutes until golden and soft. Stir in the porcini pieces or mushrooms and cook for a further 2–3 minutes. Add the sun-dried tomatoes, sausage or salami, wine, passata and stock to the pan, and bring to the boil, then reduce the heat and simmer for 10 minutes.

3. Lift the lamb from the roasting tin, add to the tomato sauce and cover with a tight-fitting lid. Reduce the oven temperature to 170°C (150°C fan oven) mark 3. Put the casserole into the oven and cook the stew for 3 hours or until the lamb is falling off the bone.

4. Lift the lamb from the casserole and put on to a deep, heatproof serving dish. Cover loosely with foil and keep warm in a low oven.

5. Put the casserole on the hob, stir in the pasta and bring back to the boil. Reduce the heat and simmer for 10 minutes or until the pasta is tender. Stir in the Parmesan just before serving. Carve the lamb into large pieces and serve with the pasta sauce, garnished with parsley.

COOK'S TIP
Look out for bags of dried porcini pieces in supermarkets. These chopped dried mushrooms are ideal for adding a rich depth of flavour to stews or casseroles.

Turkish Lamb Stew

Preparation Time 10 minutes • Cooking Time 1½–2 hours • Serves 4 • Per Serving 389 calories, 20g fat (of which 7g saturates), 28g carbohydrate, 1.2g salt • Easy

2 tbsp olive oil
400g (14oz) lean lamb fillet, cubed
1 red onion, sliced
1 garlic clove, crushed
1 potato, quartered
400g can chopped plum tomatoes
1 red pepper, seeded and sliced
200g (7oz) canned chickpeas,
    drained and rinsed
1 aubergine, cut into chunks
200ml (7fl oz) lamb stock
1 tbsp red wine vinegar
1 tsp each freshly chopped thyme,
    rosemary and oregano
8 black olives, halved and pitted
salt and ground black pepper

1. Heat 1 tbsp oil in a flameproof casserole and brown the lamb over a high heat. Reduce the heat and add the remaining oil, the onion and garlic, then cook until soft.

2. Preheat the oven to 170°C (150°C fan oven) mark 3. Add the potato, tomatoes, red pepper, chickpeas, aubergine, stock, vinegar and herbs to the pan. Season, stir and bring to the boil. Cover the pan, transfer to the oven and cook for 1–1½ hours until the lamb is tender.

3. About 15 minutes before the end of the cooking time, add the olives.

Luxury Lamb & Leek Hotpot

Preparation Time 20 minutes • Cooking Time 2 hours 50 minutes • Serves 6 • Per Serving 530 calories, 33g fat (of which 20g saturates), 27g carbohydrate, 0.5g salt • Easy

50g (2oz) butter
400g (14oz) leeks, sliced
1 medium onion, chopped
1 tbsp olive oil
800g (1lb 12oz) casserole lamb, cubed and tossed with 1 tbsp plain flour
2 garlic cloves, crushed
800g (1lb 12oz) waxy potatoes, such as Desiree, sliced
3 tbsp freshly chopped flat-leafed parsley
1 tsp freshly chopped thyme
300ml (½ pint) lamb stock
142ml carton double cream
salt and ground black pepper

1. Melt half the butter in a 3.5 litre (6¼ pint) flameproof casserole. Add the leeks and onion, stir to coat, then cover and cook over a low heat for 10 minutes.

2. Transfer the leeks and onion to a large sheet of greaseproof paper. Add the oil to the casserole and heat, then brown the meat in batches with the garlic and plenty of seasoning. Remove and put to one side on another large sheet of greaseproof paper.

3. Preheat the oven to 170°C (150°C fan oven) mark 3. Put half the potatoes in a layer over the bottom of the casserole and season with salt and pepper. Add the meat, then spoon the leek mixture on top. Arrange a layer of overlapping potatoes on top of that, sprinkle with herbs, then pour in the stock.

4. Bring the casserole to the boil, then cover and transfer to a low shelf in the oven and cook for about 1 hour 50 minutes. Remove from the oven, dot with the remaining butter and add the cream. Return to the oven and cook, uncovered, for 30–40 minutes until the potatoes are golden brown.

Lamb Boulangère

Preparation Time 40 minutes • Cooking Time about 2¼ hours, plus resting • Serves 6 • Per Serving 998 calories, 61g fat (of which 24g saturates), 53g carbohydrate, 0.8g salt • Easy

1.8kg (4lb) waxy potatoes such as King Edward, finely sliced
1 onion, sliced and blanched in boiling water for 2 minutes
600ml (1 pint) vegetable stock
5 garlic cloves, crushed
3 tbsp finely chopped fresh mint
2 tbsp finely chopped fresh rosemary
100g (3½oz) butter, at room temperature, plus extra to grease
1 leg of lamb, weighing around 2.3kg (5lb)
salt and ground black pepper

FOR THE RED PEPPER SALSA
3 red peppers
2 tbsp extra virgin olive oil, plus extra to drizzle
1 small red onion, finely sliced
juice of ½ lemon
1–2 tbsp baby capers, rinsed
5 fresh mint leaves, finely chopped

1. Preheat the oven to 200°C (180°C fan oven) mark 6. Butter a 4.5 litre (8 pint) roasting tin. Layer the potatoes and onion, seasoning with salt and pepper as you go. Pour the stock over them and cook in the oven for 30 minutes.

2. Put the garlic, herbs and butter into a bowl and mix well. Season generously. Put the lamb on a board and trim away any excess fat. Make six or seven deep cuts the butter mixture into the cuts, then smear the rest all over the leg. Put on a rack over the potatoes. Roast for 1 hour 40 minutes or 20 minutes per 450g (1lb).

3. Meanwhile, make the red pepper salsa. Put the peppers in a roasting tin, drizzle with a little oil and roast in the oven with the lamb for 30–40 minutes until the skins are slightly charred. Put in a bowl, cover with clingfilm and leave to cool.

4. Put the red onion in a bowl, add the lemon juice, season with salt and leave to marinate. Peel the peppers, slice the flesh and put in the bowl with any juice. Add the capers, oil and mint and season well, then stir everything together.

5. Put the lamb on a board, cover with foil and leave to rest for 10 minutes. Leave the potatoes in the oven to keep hot while you carve the lamb. Serve the sliced meat with the potatoes and red pepper salsa.

Lamb, Prune & Almond Tagine

Preparation Time 20 minutes, plus marinating • Cooking Time 2½ hours • Serves 6 • Per Serving 652 calories, 44g fat (of which 16g saturates), 31g carbohydrate, 0.6g salt • Easy

2 tsp coriander seeds
2 tsp cumin seeds
2 tsp chilli powder
1 tbsp paprika
1 tbsp ground turmeric
5 garlic cloves, chopped
6 tbsp olive oil
1.4kg (3lb) lamb leg steaks
75g (3oz) ghee or clarified butter (see Cook's Tip)
2 large onions, finely chopped
1 carrot, roughly chopped
900ml (1½ pints) lamb stock
300g (11oz) ready-to-eat prunes
4 cinnamon sticks
4 bay leaves

50g (2oz) ground almonds
12 shallots
1 tbsp honey
salt and ground black pepper
toasted blanched almonds and freshly chopped flat-leafed parsley to garnish
couscous to serve

1. Using a pestle and mortar or a blender, combine the coriander and cumin seeds, chilli powder, paprika, turmeric, garlic and 4 tbsp oil. Coat the lamb with the paste, then cover and chill for at least 5 hours.

2. Preheat the oven to 170°C (150°C fan oven) mark 3. Melt 25g (1oz) ghee or butter in a large flameproof casserole. Add the onions and carrot and cook until soft. Remove and put to one side. Fry the lamb on both sides in the remaining ghee or butter. Add a little of the stock and bring to the boil, scraping up the sediment from the bottom. Put the onions and carrot back in the casserole and add 100g (3½oz) prunes. Add the remaining stock with the cinnamon sticks, bay leaves and ground almonds. Season, cover and cook in the oven for 2 hours or until the meat is really tender.

3. Meanwhile, fry the shallots in the remaining oil and the honey until they turn a deep golden brown. Add to the casserole 30–40 minutes before the end of the cooking time.

4. Take the lamb out of the sauce and set aside. Put the casserole over the heat, bring the sauce to the boil and reduce to a thick consistency. Put the lamb back in the casserole, add the remaining prunes and bubble for 3–4 minutes. Garnish with almonds and parsley. Serve hot with couscous.

COOK'S TIP
To make clarified butter, heat butter in a pan without allowing it to colour. Skim off the foam; the solids will sink. Pour the clear butter into a bowl through a lined sieve. Leave for 10 minutes. Pour into a bowl, leaving any sediment behind. Cool. Store in a jar in the fridge for up to six months.

Beef Casserole with Black Olives

Preparation Time 20 minutes • Cooking Time 2 hours 10 minutes • Serves 6 • Per Serving 704 calories, 45g fat (of which 13g saturates), 9g carbohydrate, 3.3g salt • Easy

6 tbsp oil

1.1kg (2½lb) stewing steak, cut into 4cm (1½in) cubes

350g (12oz) unsmoked streaky bacon rashers, rind removed and sliced into thin strips

450g (1lb) onions, roughly chopped

3 large garlic cloves

2 tbsp tomato purée

125ml (4fl oz) brandy

1 tbsp plain flour

150ml (¼ pint) red wine

300ml (½ pint) beef stock

1 bouquet garni (see Cook's Tip, page 22)

225g (8oz) flat mushrooms, quartered if large

125g (4oz) black olives

fresh flat-leafed parsley sprigs to garnish (optional)

1. Heat 3 tbsp oil in a large flameproof casserole over a high heat. Brown the steak in batches until dark chestnut brown, then remove from the pan and keep warm. Add the bacon and fry until golden brown, then put to one side with the beef.

2. Add the remaining oil and cook the onions over a medium heat for 10–15 minutes until golden. Add the garlic, fry for 30 seconds, then add the tomato purée and cook, stirring, for 1–2 minutes. Add the brandy.

3. Preheat the oven to 170°C (150°C fan oven) mark 3. Bring the casserole to the boil and bubble to reduce by half, then add the flour and mix until smooth. Pour in the wine, bring back to the boil and bubble for 1 minute. Put the steak and bacon back into the casserole,

then add enough stock to barely cover the meat. Add the bouquet garni. Bring to the boil, then cover, put into the oven and cook for 1¼–1½ hours until the steak is tender. Add the mushrooms and cook for a further 4–5 minutes.

4. Just before serving, remove the bouquet garni and stir in the black olives. Serve hot, garnished with parsley if you like.

FREEZING TIP

To freeze Complete the recipe to the end of step 3. Cool quickly and put into a freezerproof container. Seal and freeze for up to one month.

To use Thaw overnight at cool room temperature. Preheat the oven to 180°C (160°C fan oven) mark 4. Bring slowly to the boil on the hob, then cover and reheat in the oven for 20–25 minutes. Complete the recipe.

Beef Stroganoff

Preparation Time 10 minutes • Cooking Time about 20 minutes • Serves 4 • Per Serving 750 calories, 60g fat (of which 35g saturates), 3g carbohydrate, 0.5g salt • Easy

700g (1½lb) rump or fillet steak, trimmed
50g (2oz) unsalted butter or 4 tbsp olive oil
1 onion, thinly sliced
225g (8oz) brown-cap mushrooms, sliced
3 tbsp brandy
1 tsp French mustard
200ml (7fl oz) crème fraîche
100ml (3½fl oz) double cream
3 tbsp freshly chopped flat-leafed parsley
salt and ground black pepper
rice or noodles to serve

1. Cut the steak into strips about 5mm (¼in) wide and 5cm (2in) long.

2. Heat half the butter or oil in a large heavy frying pan over a medium heat. Add the onion and cook gently for 10 minutes or until soft and golden. Remove with a slotted spoon and put to one side. Add the mushrooms to the pan and cook, stirring, for 2–3 minutes until golden brown; remove and put to one side.

3. Increase the heat and add the remaining butter or oil to the pan. Quickly fry the meat, in two or three batches, for 2–3 minutes, stirring constantly to ensure even browning. Remove from the pan. Add the brandy to the pan and allow it to bubble to reduce.

4. Put all the meat, onion and mushrooms back in the pan. Reduce the heat and stir in the mustard, crème fraîche and cream. Heat through, stir in most of the parsley and season with salt and pepper. Serve with rice or noodles, with the remaining parsley scattered over the top.

Beef with Beer & Mushrooms

Preparation Time 15 minutes • Cooking Time 2¾–3 hours • Serves 4 • Per Serving 450 calories, 22g fat (of which 8g saturates), 21g carbohydrate, 0.6g salt • Easy

700g (1½lb) braising steak, cut into large chunks about 5cm (2in) across
2 tsp plain gluten-free flour
2 tbsp oil
25g (1oz) butter
2 large onions, finely sliced
225g (8oz) carrots, cut into large sticks
200ml (7fl oz) Guinness
300ml (½ pint) vegetable stock
2 tsp tomato purée
2 tsp English mustard
2 tsp light muscovado sugar
225g (8oz) large field mushrooms

salt and ground black pepper
mashed potatoes and rocket leaves to serve

1. Preheat the oven to 150°C (130°C fan oven) mark 2. Toss the meat in the flour. Heat the oil and butter in a large flameproof casserole over a medium heat and sear the meat, a few pieces at a time, until brown all over. Lift out each batch as soon as it is browned and put to one side. The flavour and colour of the finished casserole depend on the meat taking on a good deep colour now. Stir the onions into the casserole and cook for about 10 minutes.

2. Return all the meat to the casserole, add the carrots, then stir in the Guinness, stock, tomato purée, mustard, sugar and plenty of seasoning. Bring to the boil and stir well, then cover tightly with foil or a lid and simmer gently in the oven for 1½ hours.

3. Stir the whole mushrooms into the casserole and return to the oven for a further 45 minutes to 1 hour until the meat is meltingly tender. Serve with mashed potatoes and rocket leaves.

Braised Beef with Bacon & Mushrooms

Preparation Time 20 minutes • Cooking Time about 3½ hours • Serves 4 • Per Serving 535 calories, 25g fat (of which 9g saturates), 29g carbohydrate, 1.6g salt • Easy

175g (6oz) smoked pancetta or smoked streaky bacon, cut into cubes

2 medium leeks, trimmed and thickly sliced

1 tbsp olive oil

450g (1lb) braising steak, cut into 5cm (2in) pieces

1 large onion, finely chopped

2 carrots and 2 parsnips, thickly sliced

1 tbsp plain flour

300ml (½ pint) red wine

1–2 tbsp redcurrant jelly

125g (4oz) chestnut mushrooms, halved

salt and ground black pepper

freshly chopped flat-leafed parsley to garnish

1. Preheat the oven to 170°C (150°C fan oven) mark 3. Fry the pancetta or bacon in a shallow flameproof casserole for 2–3 minutes until golden. Add the leeks and cook for 2 minutes or until the leeks are just beginning to colour. Remove with a slotted spoon and put to one side.

2. Heat the oil in the casserole and fry the beef pieces in batches for 2–3 minutes until a rich golden colour on all sides. Remove from the casserole and put to one side. Add the onion and fry over a gentle heat for 5 minutes or until golden. Stir in the carrots and parsnips, and fry for 1–2 minutes.

3. Put the beef back into the casserole and stir in the flour to soak up the juices. Gradually add the red wine and 300ml (½ pint) water, then stir in the redcurrant jelly. Season with pepper and bring to the boil. Cover with a tight-fitting lid and cook in the oven for 2 hours.

4. Stir in the fried leeks, pancetta and mushrooms, re-cover and cook for a further 1 hour or until everything is tender. Serve scattered with chopped flat-leafed parsley.

FREEZING TIP

To freeze Put into a freezerproof container, cool and freeze for up to three months.
To use Thaw overnight at cool room temperature. Preheat the oven to 180°C (160°C fan oven) mark 4. Bring to the boil on the hob, cover tightly and reheat in the oven for 30 minutes or until piping hot.

COOK'S TIP

Leeks can trap a lot of fine soil, so need to be washed thoroughly: trim the ends of the leaves, then cut a cross about 7.5cm (3in) into the white part and hold under cold running water.

Fish & Chips

Preparation Time 30 minutes • Cooking Time 40–50 minutes • Serves 4 • Per Serving 993 calories, 67g fat (of which 9g saturates), 64g carbohydrate, 1.6g salt • Easy

900g (2lb) Desiree, Maris Piper or King Edward potatoes, peeled
2–3 tbsp olive oil
sea salt flakes
sunflower oil to deep-fry
2 × 128g packs batter mix
1 tsp baking powder
¼ tsp salt
330ml bottle of lager
4 plaice fillets, about 225g (8oz) each, with skin on, trimmed and cut in half
plain flour to dust
salt and ground black pepper
lemon wedges and chives to garnish

FOR THE GARLIC MAYONNAISE
2 garlic cloves, crushed
8 tbsp mayonnaise
1 tsp lemon juice

1. Preheat the oven to 240°C (220°C fan oven) mark 9. Cut the potatoes into chips. Put them in a pan of lightly salted boiling water, cover and bring to the boil. Boil for 2 minutes, then drain well and turn on to kitchen paper to remove the excess moisture. Tip into a large non-stick roasting tin, toss with the olive oil and season with sea salt. Roast for 40–50 minutes until golden and cooked, turning from time to time.

2. Meanwhile, half-fill a deep-fat fryer with sunflower oil and heat to 190°C (test by frying a small cube of bread; it should brown in 20 seconds). Put the batter mix into a bowl with the baking powder and salt, and gradually whisk in the lager. Season the plaice and lightly dust with flour. Dip two of the fillets into the batter and deep-fry in the hot oil until golden. Transfer to a warmed plate and cover lightly with foil to keep warm while you deep-fry the remaining plaice fillets.

3. Mix the garlic, mayonnaise and lemon juice together in a bowl and season well. Serve the garlic mayonnaise with the plaice and chips, garnished with lemon wedges and chives.

TRY SOMETHING DIFFERENT
Instead of garlic mayonnaise, serve with one of the following.
Simple Tartare Sauce
Mix 8 tbsp mayonnaise with 1 tbsp each chopped capers and gherkins, 1 tbsp freshly chopped tarragon or chives and 2 tsp lemon juice.
Herby Lemon Mayonnaise
Fold 2 tbsp finely chopped parsley, the grated zest of ½ lemon and 2 tsp lemon juice into 8 tbsp mayonnaise.

Herby Lemon Fishcakes

Preparation Time 25 minutes, plus cooling • Cooking Time about 45 minutes • Serves 4 • Per Serving 721 calories, 42g fat (of which 7g saturates), 37g carbohydrate, 0.5g salt • Easy

900g (2lb) floury potatoes, such as Maris Piper, peeled and quartered
900g (2lb) salmon fillets
juice of 1 lemon
4 tbsp mayonnaise
a pinch of cayenne pepper
2 tbsp freshly chopped herbs, such as tarragon, basil or parsley, plus extra leaves to garnish
2 tbsp chilli oil
salt and ground black pepper
lemon wedges to garnish
green salad to serve

1. Put the potatoes into a large pan of lightly salted cold water, cover and bring to the boil. Reduce the heat and simmer for 20 minutes or until tender. Drain well, put the pan back on the heat to dry the potatoes, then mash.

2. Meanwhile, put the salmon into a pan with 600ml (1 pint) cold water and half the lemon juice. Cover and bring to the boil, then reduce the heat and simmer for 1 minute. Turn off the heat and leave to cool in the water for 20–30 minutes.

3. Preheat the oven to 200°C (180°C fan oven) mark 6. Drain the fish, remove the skin and discard, then flake the fish. Add to the potato along with the remaining lemon juice, the mayonnaise, cayenne pepper and chopped herbs. Season and mix together.

4. Line a large baking sheet with foil. Put a 7.5cm (3in) plain cooking ring on the baking sheet and fill with some of the mixture. Lift off, then repeat with the remainder of the mixture to make eight cakes. Drizzle with chilli oil and cook for 25 minutes or until golden. Garnish with herb leaves and lemon wedges, and serve with a green salad.

COOK'S TIP
If your fishcakes tend to fall apart, put them in the fridge for about 2 hours (or 30 minutes in the freezer) before cooking them.

Thai Fishcakes with Chilli Mayo

Preparation Time 25 minutes • Cooking Time 8–10 minutes • Serves 4 • Per Serving 554 calories, 44g fat
(of which 6g saturates), 17g carbohydrate, 1.3g salt • Easy

1 bunch of spring onions
2.5cm (1in) piece fresh root ginger,
  peeled and roughly chopped
1 lemongrass stalk, roughly
  chopped
20g pack fresh coriander
½ red chilli, seeded (see Cook's
  Tip, page 20), plus strips of red
  chilli to garnish
1 tsp Thai fish sauce (nam pla)
  (optional)
150ml (¼ pint) mayonnaise
75g (3oz) fresh white breadcrumbs
225g (8oz) haddock
225g (8oz) cooked and peeled
  prawns

oil for frying
2 tbsp Thai sweet chilli sauce
20g pack fresh basil, roughly
  chopped
1 fat garlic clove, crushed
  (optional)
2 limes, cut into wedges, and 120g
  bag baby leaf spinach to serve

1. Put the spring onions, ginger, lemongrass, coriander, chilli and fish sauce, if using, into a food processor and whiz to a rough paste. Add 3 tbsp mayonnaise, the breadcrumbs, haddock and prawns, and whiz for 5 seconds.

2. With wet hands, shape the mixture into eight patties, each about 5cm (2in) in diameter.

3. Heat a drizzle of oil in a non-stick frying pan. Fry the patties, in two batches, for 3–4 minutes on each side until crisp and golden.

4. Mix the sweet chilli sauce, basil and garlic, if using, into the remaining mayonnaise.

5. Serve the fishcakes garnished with red chilli strips, with lime wedges, the chilli mayo and spinach leaves.

Trout & Dill Fishcakes

Preparation Time 15 minutes • Cooking Time 25 minutes • Serves 4 • Per Serving 196 calories, 5g fat (of which 1g saturates), 27g carbohydrate, 0.1g salt • Easy

4 medium potatoes, peeled and roughly chopped
2 trout fillets
3 spring onions, finely chopped
2 dill sprigs, finely chopped
zest of 1 lemon
1 tbsp olive oil
a little plain gluten-free flour
salt
watercress to serve

1. Cook the potatoes in a pan of lightly salted boiling water for 6–8 minutes until tender. Drain, return to the pan and mash.

2. Preheat the grill to high. Grill the trout fillets for 8–10 minutes until cooked through and firm to the touch. Skin the fish, flake into pieces, removing any bones, then put into the pan with the mashed potato.

3. Add the spring onions, dill and lemon zest to the pan with the oil. Season with salt and mix well.

4. Shape the mixture into eight small patties. Dust with flour and put on a non-stick baking sheet, then grill for 3 minutes on each side. Serve the fishcakes hot, with watercress.

TRY SOMETHING DIFFERENT
Replace the trout with 225g (8oz) cooked salmon, haddock or smoked haddock: skin, flake and add at step 2.

Spanish Fish Stew

Preparation Time 20 minutes • Cooking Time 1 hour 10 minutes • Serves 4 • Per Serving 463 calories, 22g fat (of which 6g saturates), 32g carbohydrate, 1.8g salt • Easy

350g (12oz) small salad potatoes, halved
175g (6oz) chorizo sausage, skinned and roughly chopped
350g jar roasted peppers in olive oil, drained and chopped, oil reserved
1 garlic clove, crushed
2 small red onions, cut into thick wedges

175ml (6fl oz) dry white wine
300g (11oz) passata
25g (1oz) pitted black olives
450g (1lb) chunky white fish, such as cod and haddock, cut into large cubes
salt and ground black pepper
freshly chopped flat-leafed parsley to garnish

1. Preheat the oven to 170°C (150°C fan oven) mark 3. Put the potatoes, chorizo, roasted peppers, garlic, onions, wine and passata into a large flameproof casserole with 2 tbsp of the oil from the peppers. Season with salt and pepper.

2. Bring to the boil over a medium heat, then cover with a tight-fitting lid and cook in the oven for 45 minutes.

3. Add the olives and fish, and put back in the oven for 15 minutes or until the fish is opaque and completely cooked through. Spoon into warmed bowls and serve garnished with chopped parsley.

COOK'S TIP
Passata is a useful storecupboard ingredient from the Italian kitchen, which can be used in sauces and stews. It is made from ripe tomatoes that have been puréed and sieved to make a very smooth sauce.

Fish Stew

Preparation Time 15 minutes • Cooking Time about 30 minutes • Serves 4 • Per Serving 280 calories, 7g fat (of which 1g saturates), 34g carbohydrate, 0.3g salt • Easy

2 tbsp olive oil

1 onion, chopped

1 leek, trimmed and chopped

2 tsp smoked paprika

2 tbsp tomato purée

450g (1lb) cod or haddock, roughly chopped

125g (4oz) basmati rice

175ml (6fl oz) white wine

450ml (¾ pint) hot fish stock

200g (7oz) cooked and peeled king prawns

a large handful of spinach leaves

salt and ground black pepper

crusty bread to serve

1. Heat the oil in a large pan. Add the onion and leek, and fry for 8–10 minutes until they start to soften. Add the smoked paprika and tomato purée, and cook for 1–2 minutes.

2. Add the fish, rice, wine and hot stock. Bring to the boil, then cover the pan, reduce the heat and simmer for 10 minutes or until the fish is cooked through and the rice is tender.

3. Add the prawns and cook for 1 minute or until heated through. Stir in the spinach until it wilts and check the seasoning. Serve with chunks of bread.

TRY SOMETHING DIFFERENT

There are lots of alternatives to cod and haddock: try sea bass, gurnard, coley (saithe) or pollack.

Salmon Kedgeree

Preparation Time 15 minutes, plus soaking • Cooking Time 55 minutes • Serves 4 • Per Serving 490 calories, 15g fat (of which 2g saturates), 62g carbohydrate, 0.1g salt • Easy

50g (2oz) butter

700g (1½lb) onions, sliced

2 tsp garam masala

1 garlic clove, crushed

75g (3oz) split green lentils, soaked in 300ml (½ pint) boiling water for 15 minutes, then drained

750ml (1¼ pints) hot vegetable stock

225g (8oz) basmati rice

1 green chilli, seeded and finely chopped (see Cook's Tip, page 20)

350g (12oz) salmon fillet

salt and ground black pepper

1. Melt the butter in a flameproof casserole over a medium heat. Add the onions and cook for 5 minutes or until soft. Remove a third of the onions and put to one side. Increase the heat and cook the remaining onions for 10 minutes to caramelise. Remove and put to one side.

2. Put the first batch of onions back in the casserole, add the garam masala and garlic and cook, stirring, for 1 minute. Add the drained lentils and hot stock, cover the pan and cook for 15 minutes.

Add the rice and chilli, and season with salt and pepper. Bring to the boil, then cover the pan, reduce the heat and simmer for 5 minutes.

3. Put the salmon fillet on top of the rice, cover and continue to cook gently for 15 minutes or until the rice is cooked, the stock has been absorbed and the salmon is opaque.

4. Lift off the salmon and divide into flakes. Put it back in the casserole, and fork through the rice. Garnish with the reserved caramelised onion and serve.

TRY SOMETHING DIFFERENT
Instead of salmon, use undyed smoked haddock fillet.

Smoked Haddock Rarebit

Preparation Time 5 minutes • Cooking Time 10–15 minutes • Serves 4 • Per Serving 481 calories, 32g fat (of which 21g saturates), 16g carbohydrate, 3.4g salt • Easy

4 × 150g (5oz) smoked haddock fillets, skinned
4 slices bread
200g (7oz) spinach
2 large tomatoes, sliced
300g (11oz) low-fat crème fraîche
salt and ground black pepper

1. Preheat the grill. Season the haddock fillets with salt and pepper and put into a shallow ovenproof dish. Grill for 6–8 minutes until opaque and cooked through.

2. Toast the bread on both sides until golden.

3. Wash the spinach, squeeze out the water and put into a pan. Cover and cook for 1–2 minutes until starting to wilt. Tip into a bowl.

4. Top each piece of toast with a piece of fish, then add the tomato slices and spinach. Spoon the crème fraîche over the top and grill for 2–3 minutes to heat through. Season with pepper and serve immediately.

Seafood Gumbo

Preparation Time 10 minutes • Cooking Time 30 minutes • Serves 4 • Per Serving 559 calories, 23g fat (of which 3g saturates), 58g carbohydrate, 1.2g salt • Easy

125g (4oz) butter
50g (2oz) plain flour
1–2 tbsp Cajun spice mix
1 onion, chopped
1 green pepper, seeded and chopped
5 spring onions, sliced
1 tbsp freshly chopped flat-leafed parsley
1 garlic clove, crushed
1 beef tomato, chopped
125g (4oz) garlic sausage, finely sliced
75g (3oz) American easy-cook rice

1.1 litres (2 pints) vegetable stock
450g (1lb) okra, sliced
1 bay leaf
1 fresh thyme sprig
2 tsp salt
¼ tsp cayenne pepper
juice of ½ lemon
4 cloves
500g (1lb 2oz) frozen mixed seafood (containing mussels, squid and prawns), thawed and drained
ground black pepper

1. Heat the butter in a 2.5 litre (4¼–4½ pint) heavy-based pan over a low heat. Add the flour and Cajun spice and cook, stirring, for 1–2 minutes until golden brown. Add the onion, green pepper, spring onions, parsley and garlic. Cook for 5 minutes.

2. Add the tomato, garlic sausage and rice to the pan and stir well to coat. Add the stock, okra, bay leaf, thyme, salt, cayenne pepper, lemon juice and cloves. Season with black pepper. Bring to the boil, then reduce the heat and simmer, covered, for 12 minutes or until the rice is tender.

3. Add the seafood and cook for 2 minutes to heat through. Serve the gumbo in deep bowls.

COOK'S TIP

Gumbo is a traditional stew from the southern states of the USA, containing meat, vegetables and shellfish, and thickened with okra.

Quick Pad Thai

Preparation Time 12 minutes, plus soaking • Cooking Time 8 minutes • Serves 4 • Per Serving 451 calories, 13g fat (of which 3g saturates), 56g carbohydrate, 2.6g salt • Easy

250g (9oz) wide ribbon rice noodles
3 tbsp satay and sweet chilli pesto (see Cook's Tips)
125g (4oz) mangetouts, thinly sliced
125g (4oz) sugarsnap peas, thinly sliced
3 medium eggs, beaten
3 tbsp chilli soy sauce, plus extra to serve (see Cook's Tips)
250g (9oz) cooked and peeled tiger prawns
25g (1oz) dry-roasted peanuts, roughly crushed
lime wedges to serve (optional)

1. Put the noodles into a heatproof bowl, cover with boiling water and soak for 4 minutes until softened. Drain, rinse under cold water and put aside.

2. Heat a wok or large frying pan until hot, add the chilli pesto and stir-fry for 1 minute. Add the mangetouts and sugarsnap peas and cook for a further 2 minutes. Tip into a bowl. Put the pan back on the heat, add the eggs and cook, stirring, for 1 minute.

3. Add the soy sauce, prawns and noodles to the pan. Toss well and cook for 3 minutes or until piping hot. Return the vegetables to the pan and cook for a further 1 minute until heated through, then sprinkle with the peanuts. Serve with extra soy sauce, and lime wedges to squeeze over the pad Thai, if you like.

COOK'S TIPS
• *If you can't find satay and sweet chilli pesto, substitute 2 tbsp peanut butter and 1 tbsp sweet chilli sauce.*
• *Chilli soy sauce can be replaced with 2 tbsp light soy sauce and ½ red chilli, finely chopped (see Cook's Tip, page 20).*

Thai Noodles with Prawns

Preparation Time 10 minutes • Cooking Time 5 minutes • Serves 4 • Per Serving 343 calories, 11g fat (of which 2g saturates), 40g carbohydrate, 1g salt • Easy

4–6 tsp **Thai red curry paste**
175g (6oz) **medium egg noodles** (wholewheat if possible)
2 small **red onions**, chopped
1 **lemongrass stalk**, trimmed and sliced
1 fresh **red bird's-eye chilli**, seeded and finely chopped (see **Cook's Tip, page 11**)

300ml (½ pint) **reduced-fat coconut milk**
400g (14oz) **raw tiger prawns**, peeled and deveined (see **Cook's Tip, page 133**)
4 tbsp freshly chopped **coriander**, plus extra freshly torn coriander to garnish
salt and **ground black pepper**

1. Pour 2 litres (3½ pints) water into a large pan and bring to the boil. Add the curry paste, noodles, onions, lemongrass, chilli and coconut milk and bring back to the boil.

2. Add the prawns and chopped coriander, reduce the heat and simmer for 2–3 minutes until the prawns turn pink. Season with salt and pepper.

3. To serve, divide the noodles among four large bowls and sprinkle with the torn coriander.

PIES & ROASTS

Roast Chicken with Stuffing & Gravy

Preparation Time 30 minutes • Cooking Time about 1 hour 20 minutes, plus resting • Serves 5 • Per Serving 682 calories, 49g fat (of which 21g saturates), 17g carbohydrate, 1g salt • Easy

1.4kg (3lb) chicken
2 garlic cloves
1 onion, cut into wedges
2 tsp sea salt
2 tsp ground black pepper
4 sprigs each fresh parsley
   and tarragon
2 bay leaves
50g (2oz) butter, cut into cubes
salt and ground black pepper

FOR THE STUFFING
40g (1½oz) butter
1 small onion, chopped
1 garlic clove, crushed
75g (3oz) fresh white breadcrumbs
finely grated zest and juice of
   1 small lemon, halves reserved
   for the chicken
2 tbsp each freshly chopped
   flat-leafed parsley and tarragon
1 medium egg yolk

FOR THE GRAVY
200ml (7fl oz) white wine
1 tbsp Dijon mustard
450ml (¾ pint) hot chicken stock
25g (1oz) butter, mixed with 25g
   (1oz) plain flour (beurre manié)

1. Preheat the oven to 190°C (170°C fan oven) mark 5. To make the stuffing, melt the butter in a pan and fry the onion and garlic for 5–10 minutes until soft. Cool, then add the remaining ingredients, stirring in the egg yolk last. Season well with salt and pepper.

2. Put the chicken on a board, breast upwards, then put the garlic, onion, reserved lemon halves and half the salt, pepper and herb sprigs into the body cavity.

3. Lift the loose skin at the neck and fill the cavity with stuffing. Turn the bird on to its breast and pull the neck flap over the opening to cover the stuffing. Rest the wing tips across it and truss the chicken. Weigh the stuffed bird to calculate the cooking time, and allow 20 minutes per 450g (1lb), plus an extra 20 minutes.

4. Put the chicken on a rack in a roasting tin. Season, then add the remaining herbs and the bay leaves. Dot with the butter and roast, basting halfway through, until cooked and the juices run clear when the thickest part of the thigh is pierced with a skewer.

5. Put the chicken on a serving dish and cover with foil. Leave to rest while you make the gravy. Pour off all but about 3 tbsp fat from the tin, put the tin over a high heat, add the wine and boil for 2 minutes. Add the mustard and hot stock and bring back to the boil. Gradually whisk in knobs of the butter mixture until smooth, then season with salt and pepper. Carve the chicken and serve with the stuffing and gravy.

Mediterranean Roast Chicken

Preparation time 40 minutes • Cooking Time about 1 hour 25 minutes • Serves 4 • Per Serving 843 calories, 58g fat (of which 26g saturates), 42g carbohydrate, 0.9g salt • Easy

900g (2lb) floury potatoes, such as Maris Piper, peeled and cut into chunks
125g (4oz) butter, softened
4 tbsp roughly chopped sage leaves, stalks put to one side, plus extra leaves
4 tbsp roughly chopped thyme, stalks put to one side, plus extra sprigs
1.4kg (3lb) chicken
juice of 1 lemon, halves put to one side
2 fennel bulbs, cut into wedges
1 red onion, cut into wedges
salt and ground black pepper

1. Preheat the oven to 190°C (170°C fan oven) mark 5. Put the potatoes into a large pan of lightly salted cold water and bring to the boil. Cook for 5 minutes.

2. Meanwhile, put the butter into a bowl and mix in the chopped sage and thyme. Season well.

3. Lay the chicken on a board and put the lemon halves and herb stalks into the cavity. Ease your fingers under the skin of the neck end to separate the breast skin from the flesh, then push the herby butter up under the skin, reserving a little. Season well.

4. Put the chicken into a roasting tin, pour the lemon juice over it, then top with the extra sage and thyme and reserved butter. Drain the potatoes and shake in a colander to roughen their edges. Put around the chicken with the fennel and red onion. Roast for 1 hour 20 minutes or until the juices run clear when the thickest part of the thigh is pierced with a skewer. Carve and serve with the vegetables.

Roast Duck with Orange Sauce

Preparation Time 50 minutes • Cooking Time 1 hour 40 minutes, plus resting • Serves 4 • Per Serving 561 calories, 38g fat (of which 9g saturates), 20g carbohydrate, 0.5g salt • Easy

2 large oranges
2 large fresh thyme sprigs
2.3kg (5lb) duck, preferably
  with giblets
4 tbsp vegetable oil
2 shallots, chopped
1 tsp plain flour
600ml (1 pint) home-made
  chicken stock
25g (1oz) caster sugar
2 tbsp red wine vinegar
100ml (3½fl oz) fresh orange juice
100ml (3½fl oz) fruity German
  white wine
2 tbsp orange liqueur, such as
  Grand Marnier (optional)
1 tbsp lemon juice
salt and ground black pepper
glazed orange wedges (see Cook's
  Tip) to garnish
mangetouts and broccoli to serve

1. Preheat the oven to 200°C (180°C fan oven) mark 6. Using a zester, remove strips of zest from the oranges. Put half the zest into a pan of cold water, bring to the boil, drain and put to one side. Remove the pith from both oranges and cut the flesh into segments.

2. Put the thyme and unblanched orange zest inside the duck; season. Rub the skin with 2 tbsp oil, sprinkle with salt and place, breast side up, on a rack over a roasting tin. Roast, basting every 20 minutes, for 1¼–1½ hours until just cooked and the juices run clear when the thickest part of the thigh is pierced with a skewer. After 30 minutes, turn breast side down, then cook breast side up for the last 10 minutes.

3. Meanwhile, cut the gizzard, heart and neck into pieces. Heat the remaining 2 tbsp oil in a heavy-based pan, add the giblets and fry until dark brown. Add the chopped shallots and flour, and cook for 1 minute. Pour in the stock and bring to the boil, then bubble until reduced by half. Strain.

4. Put the sugar and vinegar into a heavy-based pan over a low heat until the sugar dissolves. Increase the heat and cook until it forms a dark caramel. Pour in the orange juice and stir. Cool, cover and put to one side.

5. Lift the duck off the rack and keep it warm. Skim all the fat off the juices to leave about 3 tbsp sediment. Stir the wine into the sediment, bring to the boil and bubble for 5 minutes or until syrupy. Add the stock mixture and orange mixture and bring back to the boil, then bubble until syrupy, skimming if necessary. To serve the sauce, add the blanched orange zest and segments. Add Grand Marnier, if using, and lemon juice to taste.

6. Carve the duck and garnish with glazed orange wedges. Serve with the orange sauce, mangetouts and broccoli.

COOK'S TIP
To glaze oranges, quarter them or cut into wedges, dust with a little caster sugar and grill until caramelised.

Roast Pork Loin with Rosemary & Mustard

Preparation Time 5 minutes • Cooking Time 1 hour 35 minutes • Serves 8 • Per Serving 354 calories, 13g fat (of which 4g saturates), 24g carbohydrate, 1.1g salt • Easy

2 tbsp freshly chopped rosemary
4 tbsp Dijon mustard
50ml (2fl oz) lemon juice
50g (2oz) light muscovado sugar
175g (6oz) honey
1 tbsp soy sauce
1.4kg (3lb) loin of pork, chine bone (backbone) removed, rib bones cut off and separated into individual ribs (ask the butcher to do this for you)
lemon wedges and rosemary sprigs to serve

1. Preheat the oven to 200°C (180°C fan oven) mark 6. Mix together the rosemary, mustard, lemon juice, sugar, honey and soy sauce and put to one side.

2. Put the loin into a roasting tin and cook in the oven for 40 minutes.

3. Add the ribs to the roasting tin and cook the pork for a further 40 minutes.

4. Drain off any fat and brush the pork with the mustard glaze. Put back in the oven for about 15 minutes, basting occasionally with the glaze or until well browned and tender. Serve hot or cold, garnished with rosemary and lemon.

COOK'S TIP

The sweetness of buttered parsnips makes them an ideal accompaniment to pork. Cut about 700g (1½lb) scrubbed, unpeeled parsnips into chunky lengths from the stalk to the root end. Melt 50g (2oz) butter in a deep frying pan and add the parsnips. Stir over the heat for 5–7 minutes, shaking the pan occasionally, until the parsnips are tender and have a wonderful sticky glaze.

Stuffed Leg of Lamb

Preparation Time 40 minutes • Cooking Time 3 hours–3 hours 40 minutes, plus resting • Serves 8 •
Per Serving 632 calories, 47g fat (of which 15g saturates), 1g carbohydrate, 0.4g salt • Easy

1 leg of lamb, about 2.7kg (6lb), knucklebone removed but end bone left in
2 garlic bulbs
salt and ground black pepper
Redcurrant Sauce (see Cook's Tip)

FOR THE STUFFING
25g (1oz) butter
75ml (2½fl oz) olive oil
1 small red onion, finely chopped
450g (1lb) chestnut mushrooms, finely chopped
4 tbsp freshly chopped flat-leafed parsley, 1 tbsp freshly chopped oregano and 6–8 thyme sprigs, leaves stripped

1. First make the stuffing. Melt the butter in a frying pan with 2 tbsp olive oil. Fry the onion gently for 10–15 minutes until soft. Add the chopped mushrooms and cook for 15–20 minutes – the mixture will become dryish – stirring all the time, until the mushrooms begin to turn golden brown. Add the herbs and cook for 1 minute. Season and leave to cool.

2. Preheat the oven to 190°C (170°C fan oven) mark 5. Open out the lamb and spread the stuffing over the meat. Reshape the lamb and secure with string. Put in a roasting tin and season. Roast, basting occasionally, for 2½–3 hours. About 1 hour before the end of the cooking time, rub the whole garlic bulbs with the remaining oil and put them alongside the lamb until very soft. When the lamb is cooked to your liking, transfer to a carving board, cover with a tent of foil and leave to rest. Keep the garlic warm until ready to serve.

3. Carve the lamb and garnish with the roasted garlic, broken into cloves. Serve with Redcurrant Sauce.

COOK'S TIP
Redcurrant Sauce
Pour 600ml (1 pint) fruity red wine into a small pan. Add 6 tbsp redcurrant jelly, 3 tbsp Worcestershire sauce and the juice of 1 lemon and 1 orange. Heat very gently until the jelly melts. Pour off all but 2 tbsp fat from the roasting tin. Put the tin on the hob over a low heat and stir in 2 tbsp plain flour and 2 tsp English mustard powder to make a paste. Increase the heat and pour in the wine mixture, a little at a time. Mix with a wooden spoon after each addition, scraping up any crusty bits from the bottom of the tin. Once all the wine has been incorporated, swap the spoon for a whisk and whisk until the sauce is smooth. Reduce the heat and bubble gently for 10 minutes, then pour into a warm jug to serve. Serves 8.

Roasted Venison Sausages

Preparation Time 10 minutes • Cooking Time 35 minutes • Serves 6 • Per Serving 439 calories, 32g fat (of which 12g saturates), 28g carbohydrate, 2.4g salt • Easy

12 venison sausages
2 tbsp redcurrant jelly
1 tsp lemon juice
mashed potatoes to serve

FOR THE RED ONION
**   MARMALADE**
400g (14oz) red onions, chopped
2 tbsp olive oil
4 tbsp red wine vinegar
2 tbsp demerara sugar
1 tsp juniper berries, crushed

1. Preheat the oven to 220°C (200°C fan oven) mark 7. Put the sausages into a small roasting tin. Mix together the redcurrant jelly and lemon juice and spoon over the sausages. Roast for 35 minutes, turning once.

2. Meanwhile, make the red onion marmalade. Gently fry the onions in the oil for 15–20 minutes. Add the vinegar, sugar and juniper berries, and continue cooking for 5 minutes or until the onions are really tender.

3. Serve the sausages with the red onion marmalade and mashed potatoes.

TRY SOMETHING DIFFERENT

Fried Sausages
Melt a little fat in a frying pan, add the sausages and fry for 15–20 minutes, keeping the heat low to prevent them burning and turning them once or twice to brown them evenly.

Grilled Sausages
Heat the grill to hot, put the sausages on the grill rack in the grill pan and cook until one side is lightly browned, then turn them; continue cooking and turning them frequently for 15–20 minutes, until the sausages are well browned.

Baked Sausages
Heat the oven to 200°C (180°C fan oven) mark 6. Put the sausages into a greased baking tin and cook in the centre of the oven for 30 minutes.

Kilted Sausages
Wrap rinded streaky bacon rashers around pairs of chipolatas and bake in the same way as above at 190°C (170°C fan oven) mark 5.

Sausages with Roasted Onions & Potatoes

Preparation Time 10 minutes • Cooking Time 1 hour 20 minutes • Serves 4 • Per Serving 640 calories, 40g fat (of which 12g saturates), 55g carbohydrate, 2.5g salt • Easy

900g (2lb) Desiree potatoes, cut into wedges
4 tbsp olive oil
3–4 fresh rosemary sprigs (optional)
2 red onions, each cut into eight wedges
8 sausages
salt and ground black pepper

1. Preheat the oven to 220°C (200°C fan oven) mark 7. Put the potatoes in a roasting tin – they should sit in one layer. Drizzle with the oil and season with salt and pepper. Toss well to coat the potatoes in oil, then put the rosemary on top, if using, and roast in the oven for 20 minutes.

2. Remove the roasting tin from the oven and add the onion wedges.

Toss again to coat the onions and turn the potatoes. Put the sausages in between the potatoes and onions. Return the tin to the oven for 1 hour.

3. Divide among four plates and serve immediately.

COOK'S TIP
If you can't find Desiree potatoes, use Maris Piper or King Edward.

Honey Pork with Roast Potatoes & Apples

Preparation Time 20 minutes • Cooking Time 1 hour 40 minutes, plus resting • Serves 4 • Per Serving 830 calories, 55g fat (of which 19g saturates), 40g carbohydrate, 0.4g salt • Easy

1kg (2¼lb) loin of pork, with skin and four bones
4 tbsp olive oil
25g (1oz) butter
700g (1½lb) Charlotte potatoes, scrubbed and halved
1 large onion, cut into eight wedges
1 tbsp clear honey mixed with 1 tbsp wholegrain mustard
2 Cox's Orange Pippin apples, cored and each cut into six wedges
12 fresh sage leaves
175ml (6fl oz) dry cider
salt and ground black pepper

1. Preheat the oven to 240°C (220°C fan oven) mark 9. Put the pork on a board and use a paring knife to score the skin into thin strips, cutting about halfway into the fat underneath. Rub 1 tsp salt and 2 tbsp oil over the skin and season well with pepper. Put the meat on a rack, skin side up, over a large roasting tin (or just put the pork in the tin). Roast for 25 minutes. Turn the oven down to 190°C (170°C fan oven) mark 5 and continue to roast for 15 minutes.

2. Add the remaining oil and the butter to the roasting tin. Scatter the potatoes and onion around the meat, season and continue to roast for 45 minutes.

3. Brush the meat with the honey and mustard mixture. Add the apples and sage leaves to the tin and roast for a further 15 minutes or until the pork is cooked.

4. Remove the pork from the tin and wrap completely with foil, then leave to rest for 10 minutes. Put the potatoes, onions and apples into a warmed serving dish and put back in the oven to keep warm.

5. Put the roasting tin on the hob, add the cider and stir well to make a thin gravy. Season.

6. Cut between each bone and cut the meat away from the bone. Pull the crackling away from the meat and cut into strips. Carve the joint, giving each person some crackling, and a bone to chew. Serve with the gravy and potatoes, onion and apples.

Classic Roast Beef with Yorkshire Puddings

Preparation Time 20 minutes • Cooking Time about 1½ hours, plus resting • Serves 8 • Per Serving 510 calories, 24g fat (of which 9g saturates), 16g carbohydrate, 0.5g salt • Easy

1 boned and rolled rib, sirloin,
   rump or topside of beef, about
   1.8kg (4lb)
1 tbsp plain flour
1 tbsp mustard powder
salt and ground black pepper
fresh thyme sprigs to garnish
vegetables to serve

**FOR THE YORKSHIRE
   PUDDING**
125g (4oz) plain flour
½ tsp salt
300ml (½ pint) milk
2 eggs

FOR THE GRAVY
150ml (¼ pint) red wine
600ml (1 pint) beef stock

1. Preheat the oven to 230°C (210°C fan oven) mark 8. Put the beef in a roasting tin, thickest part of the fat uppermost. Mix the flour with the mustard powder, salt and pepper. Rub the mixture over the beef.

2. Roast the beef in the middle of the oven for 30 minutes.

3. Baste the beef and reduce the oven temperature to 190°C (170°C fan oven) mark 5. Cook for a further 1 hour, approximately, basting occasionally.

4. Meanwhile, prepare the Yorkshire pudding batter. Sift the flour and salt into a bowl. Mix in half the milk, then add the eggs and season with pepper. Beat until smooth, then whisk in the rest of the milk.

5. Put the beef on a warmed carving dish, cover loosely with foil and leave to rest in a warm place. Increase the oven temperature to 220°C (200°C fan oven) mark 7.

6. Pour off about 3 tbsp fat from the roasting tin and use to grease 8–12 individual Yorkshire pudding tins. Heat in the oven for 5 minutes or until the fat is almost smoking. Pour the Yorkshire batter into the tins. Bake for 15–20 minutes until well risen, golden and crisp.

7. Meanwhile, make the gravy. Skim off any remaining fat from the roasting tin. Put the tin on the hob, add the wine and boil until syrupy. Pour in the stock and, again, boil until syrupy – there should be about 450ml (¾ pint) gravy. Taste and adjust the seasoning.

8. Carve the beef into slices. Garnish with thyme, serve with the gravy, Yorkshire puddings and vegetables of your choice.

Chicken & Leek Pie

Preparation Time 15 minutes • Cooking Time 40–45 minutes • Serves 4 • Per Serving 591 calories, 23g fat (of which 15g saturates), 54g carbohydrate, 0.3g salt • Easy

5 large potatoes, chopped into chunks

200g (7oz) crème fraîche

3 boneless chicken breasts, with skin on, about 125g (4oz) each

3 large leeks, trimmed and chopped into chunks

about 10 fresh tarragon leaves, finely chopped

salt and ground black pepper

1. Preheat the oven to 200°C (180°C fan oven) mark 6. Put the potatoes into a pan of lightly salted cold water. Cover the pan and bring to the boil, then reduce the heat and simmer for 10–12 minutes until soft. Drain and put back into the pan. Add 1 tbsp crème fraîche, season with salt and pepper and mash well.

2. Meanwhile, heat a frying pan, add the chicken, skin side down, and fry gently for 5 minutes or until the skin is golden. Turn the chicken over and fry for 6–8 minutes.

Remove the chicken from the pan and put on to a board. Tip the leeks into the pan and cook in the juices over a low heat for 5 minutes to soften.

3. Discard the chicken skin and cut the flesh into bite-size pieces (don't worry if it is not quite cooked through). Put the chicken back into the pan, stir in the remaining crème fraîche and heat for 2–3 minutes until bubbling. Stir in the tarragon and season with salt and pepper, then spoon into a 1.7 litre (3 pint) ovenproof dish and spread the mash on top.

4. Cook in the oven for 20–25 minutes until golden and heated through. Serve hot.

TRY SOMETHING DIFFERENT

• *To use leftover cooked chicken or turkey, don't fry the meat at step 2. Add it to the pan with the crème fraîche at step 3. Cook the leeks in 2 tsp olive oil.*

• *For a different flavour, make the mash with 2 large potatoes and a small celeriac, that has been peeled, cut into chunks and cooked with the potato.*

Chicken & Artichoke Pie

Preparation time 20 minutes • Cooking Time 45 minutes • Serves 4 • Per Serving 241 calories, 9g fat
(of which 5g saturates), 7g carbohydrate, 0.2g salt • Easy

**3 skinless chicken breasts, about
    350g (12oz)**
150ml (¼ pint) dry white wine
**225g (8oz) reduced-fat cream
    cheese with garlic and herbs**
400g can artichoke hearts in water
**4 sheets filo pastry, about 40g
    (1½oz), thawed if frozen**
olive oil
1 tsp sesame seeds
salt and ground black pepper
fresh thyme to garnish (optional)

1. Preheat the oven to 200°C
(180°C fan oven) mark 6. Put the
chicken and wine into a pan and
bring to the boil, then cover and
simmer for 10 minutes. Set the
chicken aside. Add the cheese to
the wine and mix until smooth.
Bring to the boil, then simmer
until thickened.

2. Cut the chicken into bite-sized
pieces. Drain and quarter the
artichokes and add to the sauce
with the chicken. Season and
mix well.

3. Put the mixture into a shallow
ovenproof dish. Brush the pastry
lightly with oil, scrunch slightly and
put on top of the chicken. Sprinkle
with sesame seeds.

4. Cook for 30–35 minutes until
crisp. Serve garnished with thyme,
if you like.

**TRY SOMETHING
DIFFERENT**
*Replace the artichoke hearts with
225g (8oz) brown-cap mushrooms,
cooked in a little water with
seasoning and lemon juice.*

Cheesy Chicken Cobbler

Preparation Time 20 minutes • Cooking Time about 20 minutes • Serves 4 • Per Serving 372 calories, 12g fat (of which 4g saturates), 42g carbohydrate, 2.2g salt • A Little Effort

200g (7oz) cooked skinless chicken breast, cut into bite-sized pieces
200g (7oz) frozen mixed vegetables
300g tin of tomato soup
175g (6oz) self-raising flour, plus extra to dust
½ tbsp baking powder
50g (2oz) mature Cheddar cheese, grated
75ml (3fl oz) milk, plus extra to brush
1 medium egg, lightly beaten
½ tbsp vegetable oil

1. Preheat the oven to 200°C (180°C fan) mark 6. In a medium bowl, stir together the cooked chicken, frozen vegetables, soup and some seasoning. Pour the mixture into a rough 1 litre (1¾ pint) shallow ovenproof dish and set aside.

2. Sift the flour, baking powder and a large pinch of salt into a large bowl. Stir in most of the cheese. Beat the milk, egg and oil together in a separate bowl.

3. Pour the milk mixture into the flour bowl and use a cutlery knife to bring it together until the dough forms clumps. Add a splash of milk if it looks too dry.

4. Tip the dough on to a lightly floured surface and pat it into a rough 9 x 15cm (3½ x 6in) rectangle. Cut the rectangle into eight equal squares, then arrange the scones on top of the chicken mixture. Brush each scone with a little milk, then sprinkle over the remaining cheese.

5. Cook in the oven for 20 minutes or until the scones are risen and golden, and the filling is bubbling and piping hot. Serve immediately.

Shepherd's Pie

Preparation Time 20 minutes • Cooking Time about 55 minutes • Serves 4 • Per Serving 513 calories, 27g fat (of which 11g saturates), 44g carbohydrate, 0.6g salt • Easy

2 tbsp sunflower oil

450g (1lb) minced lamb

1 large onion, chopped

50g (2oz) mushrooms, sliced

2 carrots, chopped

2 tbsp plain flour

1 tbsp tomato purée

1 bay leaf

300ml (½ pint) lamb stock

700g (1½lb) potatoes, cut into large chunks

25g (1oz) butter

75ml (2½fl oz) milk

50g (2oz) Lancashire or Cheddar cheese, crumbled (optional)

salt and ground black pepper

1. Heat half the oil in a large pan and brown the mince over a medium to high heat – do this in batches, otherwise the meat will steam rather than fry. Remove with a slotted spoon and put to one side.

2. Turn the heat to low and add the remaining oil. Gently fry the onion, mushrooms and carrots for 10 minutes or until softened. Stir in the flour and tomato purée and cook for 1 minute. Return the meat to the pan and add the bay leaf. Pour in the stock and bring to the boil, then cover the pan, reduce the heat and simmer for 25 minutes.

3. Preheat the oven to 200°C (180°C fan oven) mark 6. Cook the potatoes in lightly salted boiling water for 20 minutes or until tender. Drain and leave to stand in the colander for 2 minutes to steam dry. Melt the butter with the milk in the potato pan and add the cooked potatoes. Mash until smooth.

4. Spoon the lamb mixture into a 1.7 litre (3 pint) ovenproof casserole dish. Remove the bay leaf and check the seasoning. Cover with the mashed potato and sprinkle the cheese over it, if using. Bake for 15–20 minutes until bubbling and golden. Serve immediately with green vegetables.

Cottage Pie

Preparation Time 15 minutes • Cooking Time about 1 hour • Serves 4 • Per Serving 581 calories, 28g fat (of which 12g saturates), 55g carbohydrate, 1.8g salt • Easy

1 tbsp olive oil
1 onion, peeled and finely chopped
2 garlic cloves, peeled and crushed
450g (1lb) minced beef
1 tbsp plain flour
450ml (¾ pint) beef stock
2 tbsp Worcestershire sauce
1 medium carrot, peeled and diced
125g (4oz) button mushrooms, sliced
1kg (2¼lb) potatoes, roughly chopped
25g (1oz) butter
60ml (2¼fl oz) milk
salt and ground black pepper

1. Heat the oil in a large pan, add the onion and fry over a medium heat for 15 minutes until softened and golden, stirring occasionally. Add the garlic and cook for 1 minute.

2. Preheat the oven to 200°C (180°C fan oven) mark 6. Add minced beef to the onion and garlic and, as it browns, use a wooden spoon to break up the pieces. Once it's brown, stir in the flour. Stir in the stock to the browned mince, cover the pan with a lid and bring to the boil. Add the Worcestershire sauce, carrot and mushrooms and season well with salt and pepper. Reduce the heat, cover and cook for 15 minutes.

3. Meanwhile, put the potatoes into a large pan of salted water. Bring to the boil and cook for about 20–25 minutes until very soft. Drain and put back into the pan over a low heat to dry off. Mash until smooth, and then beat in the butter and milk. Season with salt and pepper to taste.

4. Spoon the sauce into a 1.7 litre (3 pint) ovenproof dish, cover with the mashed potato, then cook in the oven for 20–25 minutes or until piping hot and the topping is golden brown.

TRY SOMETHING DIFFERENT
To make individual pies, use four 450ml (¾ pint) shallow ovenproof dishes.

Steak & Onion Puff Pie

Preparation Time 30 minutes • Cooking Time about 2½ hours • Serves 4 • Per Serving 1036 calories, 67g fat (of which 10g saturates), 65g carbohydrate, 1.4g salt • Easy

3 tbsp vegetable oil
2 onions, sliced
900g (2lb) casserole beef, cut into chunks
3 tbsp plain flour
500ml (18fl oz) hot beef stock
2 fresh rosemary sprigs, bruised
flour to dust
500g pack puff pastry
1 medium egg, beaten, to glaze
salt and ground black pepper

1. Preheat the oven to 170°C (150°C fan oven) mark 3.

2. Heat 1 tbsp oil in a large flameproof casserole and sauté the onions for 10 minutes or until golden. Lift out and put to one side. Sear the meat in the same casserole, in batches, using more oil as necessary, until brown all over. Lift out each batch as soon as it is browned and put to one side. Add the flour to the casserole and cook for 1–2 minutes to brown. Return the onions and beef to the casserole and add the hot stock and the rosemary. Season well with salt and pepper. Cover and bring to the boil, then cook in the oven for 1½ hours or until the meat is tender.

3. About 30 minutes before the end of the cooking time, lightly dust a worksurface with flour and roll out the pastry. Cut out a lid using a 1.1 litre (2 pint) pie dish as a template, or use four 300ml (½ pint) dishes and cut out four lids. Put on a baking sheet and chill.

4. Remove the casserole from the oven. Increase the heat to 220°C (200°C fan oven) mark 7. Pour the casserole into the pie dish (or dishes), brush the edge with water and put on the pastry lid. Press lightly to seal. Lightly score the top and brush with the egg. Put the dish back on the baking sheet. Bake for 30 minutes or until the pastry is risen and golden. Serve immediately.

FREEZING TIP

To freeze Complete recipe to the end of step 3. Cool the casserole quickly. Put the beef mixture into a pie dish. Brush the dish edge with water, put on the pastry and press down lightly to seal. Score the pastry. Cover with clingfilm and freeze for up to three months.
To use Thaw overnight at cool room temperature or in the fridge. Lightly score the pastry, brush with beaten egg and cook at 220°C (200°C fan oven) mark 7 for 35 minutes or until the pastry is brown and the filling piping hot.

Steak & Kidney Pie

Preparation Time 40 minutes, plus cooling • Cooking Time about 1½ hours • Serves 6 • Per Serving 565 calories, 36g fat (of which 8g saturates), 26g carbohydrate, 0.9g salt • Easy

700g (1½lb) stewing steak, cut into cubes and seasoned
2 tbsp plain flour, plus extra to dust
3 tbsp vegetable oil
25g (1oz) butter
1 small onion, finely chopped
175g (6oz) ox kidney, cut into small pieces
150g (5oz) flat mushrooms, cut into large chunks
a small pinch of cayenne pepper
1 tsp anchovy essence
350g (12oz) puff pastry, thawed if frozen
1 large egg, beaten with a pinch of salt, to glaze
salt and ground black pepper

1. Preheat the oven to 170°C (150°C fan oven) mark 3. Toss half the steak with half the flour. Heat the oil in a flameproof non-stick casserole and add the butter. Fry the steak in batches until brown. Lift out each batch as soon as it is browned and put to one side.

2. Add the onion and cook gently until soft. Return the steak to the casserole with 200ml (7fl oz) water, the kidney, mushrooms, cayenne and anchovy essence. Bring to the boil, then cover the pan, reduce the heat and simmer for 5 minutes.

3. Transfer to the oven and cook for 1 hour or until tender. The sauce should be syrupy. If not, transfer the casserole to the hob, remove the lid, bring to the boil and bubble for 5 minutes to reduce the liquid. Leave the steak mixture to cool.

4. Preheat the oven to 200°C (180°C fan oven) mark 6. Put the steak and kidney mixture into a 900ml (1½ pint) pie dish. Pile it high to support the pastry lid.

5. Roll out the pastry on a lightly floured surface to 5mm (¼in) thick. Cut off four to six strips, 1cm (½in) wide. Dampen the edge of the dish with cold water, then press the pastry strips on to the edge.

Dampen the pastry rim and lay the sheet of pastry on top. Press the surfaces together, trim the edge and press down with the back of a knife to seal. Brush the pastry with the glaze and score with the back of a knife. Put the pie dish on a baking sheet and cook for 30 minutes or until the pastry is golden brown and the filling is hot to the centre.

Luxury Smoked Fish Pie

Preparation Time 30 minutes • Cooking Time 1 hour 20 minutes • Serves 4 • Per Serving 1057 calories, 63g fat (of which 34g saturates), 66g carbohydrate, 3.8g salt • Easy

- **1.1kg (2½lb) Desiree potatoes, peeled and cut into rough chunks**
- **450ml (¾ pint) milk**
- **125g (4oz) butter**
- **125g (4oz) Cheddar cheese, grated**
- **75ml (2½fl oz) dry white wine**
- **150ml (¼ pint) fish stock**
- **450g (1lb) skinless smoked haddock fillet, undyed if possible, cut into wide strips**
- **350g (12oz) skinless salmon fillet, cut into wide strips**
- **40g (1½oz) plain flour**
- **75ml (2½fl oz) double cream**
- **1 tbsp capers, drained, rinsed and chopped**
- **1½ tbsp freshly chopped flat-leafed parsley**
- **2 medium eggs, hard-boiled**
- **salt and ground black pepper**

1. Preheat the oven to 180°C (160°C fan oven) mark 4. Put the potatoes into a pan of lightly salted water and bring to the boil, then cover the pan, reduce the heat and simmer until tender.

2. Warm 100ml (3½fl oz) milk. Drain the potatoes, then put back into the pan over a low heat for 2 minutes. Mash until smooth. Stir in 75g (3oz) butter, half the cheese and the warmed milk, then season with salt and pepper. Cover and put to one side.

3. Meanwhile, bring the wine, stock and remaining milk to the boil in a large wide pan. Add the haddock and salmon and return the liquid to the boil, then reduce the heat to poach the fish gently for 5 minutes or until it flakes easily. Lift the fish with a draining spoon into a 1.4 litre (2½ pint) deep ovenproof dish and flake with a fork if necessary. Put the cooking liquid to one side.

4. Melt the remaining butter in another pan, add the flour and stir until smooth, then cook for 2 minutes. Gradually add the fish liquid, whisking until smooth. Bring to the boil, stirring, and cook for 2 minutes or until thickened. Stir in the cream, capers and parsley and season to taste with salt and pepper.

5. Shell the eggs and chop roughly. Scatter over the fish, then pour in the sauce. Spoon the potato mixture on top, then sprinkle with the remaining cheese.

6. Bake the pie for 35–40 minutes until golden and bubbling at the edges. Serve hot.

Seafood Pie with Blue Cheese

Preparation Time 40 minutes • Cooking Time about 1 hour • Serves 4 • Per Serving 634 calories, 32g fat
(of which 20g saturates), 42g carbohydrate, 1.5g salt • Easy

**450g (1lb) cod, haddock or
whiting fillet**
50ml (2fl oz) milk
**25g (1oz) butter, plus extra
to grease**
**350g (12oz) leeks, trimmed
and sliced**
freshly grated nutmeg
**225g (8oz) large raw prawns, peeled
and deveined (see Cook's Tips)**
**Blue Cheese Sauce (see Cook's
Tips)**
**700g (1½lb) floury potatoes, cut
into 5mm (¼in) slices, boiled for
5 minutes, then drained**
salt and ground black pepper

1. Put the fish into a shallow pan
and pour the milk over it. Season
lightly with salt and pepper, cover
and poach for about 5 minutes or
until the fish flakes easily. Strain,
reserving the cooking liquid. Flake
the fish, discarding the skin and
bones, and put to one side.

2. Melt the butter in a pan and fry
the leeks for 3 minutes adding
plenty of nutmeg. Lightly butter a
1.7 litre (3 pint) pie dish. Preheat
the oven to 190°C (170°C fan oven)
mark 5.

3. Mix the fish, leeks and prawns
together in the prepared pie dish.
Spoon half the cheese sauce over
the top. Layer the cooked potato
slices over the filling, then pour the
remaining sauce over the potatoes.
Place the dish on a baking sheet
and bake for 45 minutes or until the
pie is bubbling and golden.

COOK'S TIPS

• To devein prawns, use a small
sharp knife to make a shallow cut
along the back of the prawn. Using
the point of the knife, remove and
discard the black vein (the intestinal
tract) that runs along the back of
the prawn.

Blue Cheese Sauce
*Melt 50g (2oz) butter in a small pan.
Add 3 tbsp plain flour and cook,
stirring, for 1 minute. Remove from
the heat and gradually stir in 350ml
(12fl oz) milk. (Alternatively, use
300ml (½ pint) milk and the
reserved fish poaching liquid.)
Return the pan to a gentle heat and
cook the sauce, stirring, until
thickened and smooth. Crumble in
125g (4oz) Stilton cheese, then stir in
4 tbsp single cream and season with
salt and pepper.*

Smoked Haddock & Potato Pie

Preparation Time 15 minutes • Cooking Time 1¼ hours–1 hour 25 minutes • Serves 4 • Per Serving 380 calories, 20g fat (of which 11g saturates), 37g carbohydrate, 1.5g salt • Easy

142ml carton double cream
150ml (¼ pint) fish stock
3 medium baking potatoes, thinly sliced
300g (11oz) skinless smoked haddock fillets, roughly chopped
20g pack fresh chives, chopped
1 large onion, finely chopped
salt and ground black pepper
green salad to serve

1. Preheat the oven to 200°C (180°C fan oven) mark 6. Pour the cream into a large bowl. Add the fish stock and stir well to combine.

2. Add the potatoes, haddock, chives and onion and season with salt and pepper. Toss everything together to coat. Spoon the mixture into a shallow 2.4 litre (4¼ pint) ovenproof dish.

3. Cover the dish with foil, put it on a baking tray and cook for 45 minutes. Remove the foil and cook for 30–40 minutes until bubbling and the top is golden.

4. To check that the potatoes are cooked, insert a skewer or small knife – it should push in easily. If you like, you can put the dish under a hot grill to make the top layer crisp. Leave to cool slightly, then serve with a green salad.

COOK'S TIP
For the lightest texture, make sure you use floury baking potatoes, as salad potatoes are too waxy.

HOT & SPICY

Chicken, Bean & Spinach Curry

Preparation Time 10 minutes • Cooking Time about 20 minutes • Serves 4 • Per Serving 364 calories, 9g fat (of which 1g saturates), 41g carbohydrate, 2.9g salt • Easy

1 tbsp sunflower oil
350g (12oz) skinless chicken breasts, cut into strips
1 garlic clove, crushed
300–350g tub or jar curry sauce
400g can aduki beans, drained and rinsed
175g (6oz) ready-to-eat dried apricots
150g (5oz) natural bio yogurt, plus extra to serve
125g (4oz) ready-to-eat baby spinach
naan bread to serve

1. Heat the oil in a large pan over a medium heat and fry the chicken strips with the garlic until golden. Add the curry sauce, beans and apricots, then cover and simmer gently for 15 minutes or until the chicken is tender.

2. Over a low heat, stir in the yogurt, keeping the curry hot without boiling it, then stir in the spinach until it just begins to wilt. Serve immediately with naan bread.

TRY SOMETHING DIFFERENT
Use pork escalopes cut into thin strips instead of chicken.

Hot Jungle Curry

Preparation Time 10 minutes • Cooking Time 18–20 minutes • Serves 4 • Per Serving 160 calories, 5g fat
(of which 1g saturates), 5g carbohydrate, 1.1g salt • Easy

1 tbsp vegetable oil

350g (12oz) boneless, skinless chicken breasts, cut into 5cm (2in) strips

2 tbsp Thai red curry paste

2.5cm (1in) piece fresh root ginger, peeled and thinly sliced

125g (4oz) aubergine, cut into bite-size pieces

125g (4oz) baby sweetcorn, halved lengthways

75g (3oz) green beans, trimmed

75g (3oz) button or brown-cap mushrooms, halved if large

2–3 kaffir lime leaves (optional)

450ml (¾ pint) chicken stock

2 tbsp Thai fish sauce (nam pla)

grated zest of ½ lime, plus extra to garnish

1 tsp tomato purée

1 tbsp soft brown sugar

1. Heat the oil in a wok or large frying pan. Add the chicken and cook, stirring, for 5 minutes or until the chicken turns golden brown.

2. Add the red curry paste and cook for a further 1 minute. Add the ginger, aubergine, sweetcorn, beans, mushrooms and lime leaves, if using, and stir until coated in the red curry paste. Add all the remaining ingredients and bring to the boil. Reduce the heat and simmer gently for 10–12 minutes until the chicken and vegetables are just tender. Serve immediately, sprinkled with lime zest.

TRY SOMETHING DIFFERENT

Add a drained 225g can of bamboo shoots with the other vegetables in step 2, if you like.

Thai Green Curry

Preparation Time 10 minutes • Cooking Time 15 minutes • Serves 6 • Per Serving 132 calories, 2g fat (of which 0g saturates), 4g carbohydrate, 1.4g salt • Easy

2 tsp vegetable oil
1 green chilli, seeded and finely chopped (see Cook's Tip, page 20)
4cm (1½in) piece fresh root ginger, peeled and finely grated
1 lemongrass stalk, trimmed and cut into three pieces
225g (8oz) brown-cap or oyster mushrooms
1 tbsp Thai green curry paste
300ml (½ pint) coconut milk
150ml (¼ pint) chicken stock
1 tbsp Thai fish sauce (nam pla)
1 tsp light soy sauce
350g (12oz) boneless, skinless chicken breasts, cut into bite-size pieces
350g (12oz) cooked peeled large prawns
fresh coriander sprigs to garnish
Thai fragrant rice to serve

1. Heat the oil in a wok or large frying pan, add the chilli, ginger, lemongrass and mushrooms, and stir-fry for about 3 minutes or until the mushrooms begin to turn golden. Add the curry paste and fry for a further 1 minute.

2. Pour in the coconut milk, stock, fish sauce and soy sauce and bring to the boil. Stir in the chicken, then reduce the heat and simmer for about 8 minutes or until the chicken is cooked.

3. Add the prawns and cook for a further 1 minute. Garnish with coriander sprigs and serve immediately, with Thai fragrant rice.

Spiced Chicken

Preparation Time 10 minutes, plus marinating • Cooking Time 1 hour 10 minutes • Serves 6 • Per Serving
604 calories, 36g fat (of which 10g saturates), 20g carbohydrate, 0.5g salt • Easy

3 tbsp Thai red curry paste
150ml (¼ pint) orange juice
2 garlic cloves, crushed
6 chicken pieces, 2.3kg (5lb) total
   weight, with bone in
700g (1½lb) squash or pumpkin,
   peeled and cut into 5cm (2in)
   cubes
5 red onions, quartered
2 tbsp capers, drained and chopped
salt and ground black pepper

1. Combine the curry paste, orange juice and garlic in a bowl. Put the chicken pieces in the marinade and leave to marinate for 15 minutes.

2. Preheat the oven to 220°C (200°C fan oven) mark 7. Put the vegetables into a large roasting tin, then remove the chicken from the marinade and arrange on top of the vegetables. Pour the marinade over it and season with salt and pepper. Mix everything together, so that it's covered with the marinade, then scatter with the capers.

3. Cook for 1 hour 10 minutes, turning from time to time, or until the chicken is cooked through and the skin is golden.

GET AHEAD
To prepare ahead Complete the recipe to the end of step 2. Cover and chill for up to one day.
To use Complete the recipe, but cook for a further 5–10 minutes.

Moroccan Chicken with Chickpeas

Preparation Time 10 minutes • Cooking Time 50 minutes • Serves 6 • Per Serving 440 calories, 18g fat (of which 6g saturates), 33g carbohydrate, 1g salt • Easy

12 chicken pieces, including thighs, drumsticks and breast
25g (1oz) butter
1 large onion, sliced
2 garlic cloves, crushed
2 tbsp harissa paste
a generous pinch of saffron
1 tsp salt
1 cinnamon stick
600ml (1 pint) chicken stock
75g (3oz) raisins
2 × 400g cans chickpeas, drained and rinsed
ground black pepper
plain naan or pitta bread to serve

1. Heat a large wide non-stick pan. Add the chicken pieces and fry until well browned all over. Add the butter and, when melted, add the onion and garlic. Cook, stirring, for 5 minutes.

2. Add the harissa, saffron, salt and cinnamon stick, then season well with pepper. Pour in the stock and bring to the boil. Reduce the heat, cover and simmer gently for 25–30 minutes.

3. Add the raisins and chickpeas, and bring to the boil, then reduce the heat and simmer uncovered for 5–10 minutes.

4. Serve with warm flat bread such as plain naan or pitta.

GET AHEAD
To prepare ahead *Complete the recipe, then cool quickly. Put into a sealable container and freeze for up to three months.*
To use *Thaw overnight in the fridge. Put into a pan, cover and bring to the boil. Reduce the heat to low, then reheat for 40 minutes or until the chicken is hot right through. Instead of bread, serve with couscous or brown rice.*

Spiced Chicken Pilau

Preparation Time 15 minutes • Cooking Time 35–40 minutes • Serves 4 • Per Serving 649 calories, 18g fat (of which 2g saturates), 87g carbohydrate, 2.8g salt • Easy

50g (2oz) pinenuts

2 tbsp olive oil

2 onions, sliced

2 garlic cloves, crushed

2 tbsp medium curry powder

6 boneless, skinless chicken thighs or 450g (1lb) skinless cooked chicken, cut into strips

350g (12oz) American easy-cook rice

2 tsp salt

a pinch of saffron

50g (2oz) sultanas

225g (8oz) ripe tomatoes, roughly chopped

1. Spread the pinenuts over a baking sheet and toast under a hot grill until golden brown, turning them frequently. Put to one side.

2. Heat the oil in a large heavy-based pan over a medium heat. Add the onions and garlic, and cook for 5 minutes until soft. Remove half the onion mixture and put to one side.

3. Add the curry powder and cook for 1 minute, then add the chicken and stir. Cook for 10 minutes if the meat is raw, or for 4 minutes if you're using cooked chicken, stirring from time to time until browned.

4. Add the rice, stir to coat in the oil, then add 900ml (1½ pints) boiling water, the salt and saffron. Cover and bring to the boil. Reduce the heat to low and cook for 20 minutes or until the rice is tender and most of the liquid has been absorbed. Stir in the reserved onion mixture, the sultanas, tomatoes and pinenuts. Cook for 5 minutes to warm through, then serve.

TRY SOMETHING DIFFERENT
This is also a good way to use leftover roast turkey.

Beef Jambalaya

Preparation Time 10 minutes • Cooking Time 40 minutes • Serves 4 • Per Serving 554 calories, 30g fat (of which 9g saturates), 40g carbohydrate, 1.8g salt • Easy

275g (10oz) fillet steak, cut into thin strips

4 tsp mild chilli powder

1 tsp ground black pepper

about 5 tbsp oil

150g (5oz) chorizo sausage, sliced and cut into strips, or 125g (4oz) cubed sausage

2 celery sticks, cut into 5cm (2in) strips

2 red peppers, cut into 5cm (2in) strips

150g (5oz) onions, roughly chopped

2 garlic cloves, crushed

275g (10oz) long-grain white rice

1 tbsp tomato purée

1 tbsp ground ginger

2 tsp Cajun seasoning

900ml (1½ pints) beef stock

8 large cooked prawns, peeled and deveined (see Cook's Tip, page 133)

salt

mixed salad to serve

1. Put the steak into a plastic bag with 1 tsp chilli powder and the black pepper, seal and shake to mix.

2. Heat 1 tbsp oil in a large heavy-based frying pan and cook the chorizo or sausage until golden. Add the celery and peppers to the pan and cook for 3–4 minutes until just beginning to soften and brown. Remove from the pan and put to one side. Add 2 tbsp of the oil to the pan and fry the steak in batches; put to one side and keep warm.

3. Add a little more oil to the pan, if needed, and cook the onions until transparent. Add the garlic, rice, tomato purée, remaining chilli powder, ground ginger and Cajun seasoning, then cook for 2 minutes until the rice turns translucent.

4. Stir in the stock, season with salt and bring to the boil. Cover and simmer for about 20 minutes, stirring occasionally, until the rice is tender and most of the liquid has been absorbed (add a little more water during cooking if needed).

5. Add the reserved steak, chorizo, red peppers and celery and the prawns. Heat gently, stirring, until piping hot. Adjust the seasoning and serve with a mixed salad.

COOK'S TIP

Jambalaya is a rice-based dish from Louisiana that traditionally contains spicy sausage, chicken, ham or prawns and lots of chilli pepper.

Spicy Beef

Preparation Time 10 minutes • Cooking Time 40 minutes • Serves 4 • Per Serving 487 calories, 21g fat
(of which 8g saturates), 45g carbohydrate, 1.8g salt • Easy

2 tsp sunflower oil
1 large onion, roughly chopped
1 garlic clove, finely chopped
**1 small fresh red chilli, finely
    chopped (see Cook's Tip,
    page 20)**
**2 red peppers, seeded and
    roughly chopped**
2 celery sticks, diced
400g (14oz) lean beef mince
400g can chopped tomatoes
**2 × 400g cans mixed beans, drained
    and rinsed**
1–2 tsp Tabasco sauce
**2–3 tbsp roughly chopped fresh
    coriander to garnish (optional)**
**salsa (see Cook's Tip) and soft flour
    tortillas or basmati rice to serve**

1. Heat the oil in a large heavy-based frying pan over a medium heat. Add the onion to the pan with 2 tbsp water and cook for 10 minutes or until soft. Add the garlic and chilli and cook for a further 1–2 minutes until golden Add the red peppers and celery, and cook for 5 minutes.

2. Add the beef to the pan and brown all over. Add the tomatoes, beans and Tabasco sauce, then simmer for 20 minutes. Garnish with coriander, if you like, and serve with salsa and tortillas or rice.

COOK'S TIP
To make a quick salsa, peel and roughly chop ½ ripe avocado. Put into a bowl with 4 roughly chopped tomatoes, 1 tsp olive oil and the juice of ½ lime. Mix well.

Mexican Chilli Con Carne

Preparation Time 5 minutes • Cooking Time about 1 hour • Serves 4 • Per Serving 408 calories, 19g fat
(of which 7g saturates), 28g carbohydrate, 1.1g salt • Easy

2 tbsp olive oil

450g (1lb) minced beef

1 large onion, finely chopped

1 tsp each hot chilli powder and
    ground cumin

3 tbsp tomato purée

300ml (½ pint) hot vegetable stock

400g can chopped tomatoes with
    garlic (see Cook's Tips)

25g (1oz) dark chocolate

400g can red kidney beans, drained
    and rinsed

2 × 20g packs fresh coriander,
    chopped

salt and ground black pepper

guacamole, salsa (see Cook's Tip,
    page 145), soured cream, grated
    cheese, tortilla chips and
    pickled chillies to serve

COOK'S TIPS

• *Instead of a can of tomatoes
with garlic, use a can of chopped
tomatoes and 1 crushed garlic
clove.*

• *Adding a little dark chocolate
to chilli con carne brings out
the flavours of this tasty dish.*

1. Heat 1 tbsp oil in a large
non-stick pan and fry the beef
for 10 minutes until well browned,
stirring to break up any lumps.
Remove from the pan with a
slotted spoon and set aside.

2. Add the remaining oil to the
pan, then fry the onion, stirring,
for 10 minutes or until soft and
golden.

3. Add the spices and fry for
1 minute, then return the beef to
the pan. Add the tomato purée, hot
stock and tomatoes. Bring to the
boil, then reduce the heat to a
simmer. Continue to bubble gently,
uncovered, for 35–40 minutes, or
until the sauce is well reduced and
the mixture is quite thick.

4. Stir in the chocolate, kidney
beans and coriander, season with
salt and pepper, then simmer for
5 minutes.

5. Serve with guacamole, salsa,
soured cream, grated cheese,
tortilla chips and pickled chillies.

Sweet Chilli Beef Stir-fry

Preparation Time 10 minutes • Cooking Time 10–15 minutes • Serves 4 • Per Serving 273 calories, 13g fat (of which 5g saturates), 8g carbohydrate, 0.2g salt • Easy

1 tsp chilli oil

1 tbsp each tamari (wheat-free Japanese soy sauce) and clear honey

1 garlic clove, crushed

1 large red chilli, seeded and chopped (see Cook's Tip, page 20)

400g (14oz) lean beef, cut into strips

1 tsp sunflower oil

1 broccoli head, in small florets

200g (7oz) mangetouts, halved

1 red pepper, halved, seeded and cut into strips

rice to serve

1. Pour the chilli oil into a medium-sized shallow bowl. Add the tamari, honey, garlic and chilli and stir well. Add the strips of beef and toss in the marinade.

2. Heat the sunflower oil in a wok over a high heat until it is very hot. Cook the strips of beef in two batches, for 3–4 minutes until just cooked through, then take them out of the wok and put to one side. Wipe the wok with kitchen paper to remove any residue.

3. Add the broccoli, mangetouts, red pepper and 2 tbsp water, and stir-fry for 5–6 minutes until starting to soften. Return the beef to the wok to heat through. Serve with rice.

TRY SOMETHING DIFFERENT

Use pork fillet instead of beef, trimmed of fat and cut into thin slices.

Thai Beef Curry

Preparation Time 20 minutes, plus cooling • Cooking Time about 30 minutes • Serves 4 • Per Serving 443 calories, 26g fat (of which 7g saturates), 23g carbohydrate, 1.2g salt • A Little Effort

4 cloves
1 tsp coriander seeds
1 tsp cumin seeds
seeds from 3 cardamom pods
2 garlic cloves, roughly chopped
2.5cm (1in) piece fresh root ginger, peeled and roughly chopped
1 small onion, roughly chopped
2 tbsp sunflower oil
1 tbsp sesame oil
1 tbsp Thai red curry paste
1 tsp turmeric
450g (1lb) sirloin steak, cut into 3cm (1¼in) cubes
225g (8oz) potatoes, quartered
4 tomatoes, quartered
1 tsp sugar
1 tbsp light soy sauce
300ml (½ pint) coconut milk
150ml (¼ pint) beef stock
4 small red chillies, bruised (see Cook's Tip, page 20)
50g (2oz) cashew nuts
rice and stir-fried green vegetables to serve

1. Put the cloves, coriander, cumin and cardamom seeds into a small heavy-based frying pan and fry over a high heat for 1–2 minutes until the spices release their aroma. Be careful that they do not burn. Leave to cool slightly, then grind to a powder in a spice grinder or blender.

2. Put the garlic, ginger and onion into a blender or food processor and whiz to form a smooth paste. Heat the sunflower and sesame oils in a wok or deep frying pan. Add the onion purée and the curry paste and stir-fry for 5 minutes, then add the ground roasted spices and the turmeric and fry for a further 5 minutes.

3. Add the beef to the pan and fry for 5 minutes or until browned on all sides. Add the potatoes, tomatoes, sugar, soy sauce, coconut milk, stock and chillies. Bring to the boil, then reduce the heat, cover the pan and simmer gently for about 15 minutes or until the beef is tender and the potatoes are cooked.

4. Stir in the cashew nuts and serve the curry with rice and stir-fried vegetables.

Smoky Pimento Goulash

Preparation Time 20 minutes • Cooking Time about 3 hours • Serves 8 • Per Serving 515 calories, 35g fat
(of which 14g saturates), 13g carbohydrate, 1.3g salt • Easy

1.1kg (2½lb) braising steak
3 tbsp olive oil
16 shallots or button onions
225g (8oz) piece chorizo sausage,
  roughly chopped
1 red chilli, seeded and finely
  chopped (see Cook's Tip, page 20)
3 bay leaves
3 garlic cloves, crushed
2 tbsp plain flour
2 tbsp smoked paprika
700g jar tomato passata
100ml (3½fl oz) hot beef stock
salt and ground black pepper
mashed potatoes and green
  vegetables to serve

FOR THE MINTED SOURED
CREAM
284ml carton soured cream
1 tbsp finely chopped fresh mint
1 tbsp extra virgin olive oil, plus
  extra to drizzle

1. Mix together all the ingredients for the minted soured cream and season with a little salt and plenty of coarsely ground black pepper. Cover and chill until needed.

2. Preheat the oven to 170°C (150°C fan oven) mark 3. Cut the braising steak into large cubes, slightly larger than bite-size.

3. Heat the oil in a 4 litre (7 pint) flameproof casserole until really hot. Brown the beef, a few cubes at a time, over a high heat until deep brown all over. Remove with a slotted spoon; set aside. Repeat with the remaining beef until all the pieces have been browned.

4. Reduce the heat under the casserole, then add the onions, chorizo, chilli, bay leaves and garlic. Fry for 7–10 minutes until the onions are golden brown and beginning to soften. Return the meat to the casserole and stir in the flour and paprika. Cook, stirring, for 1–2 minutes, then add the passata. Season, cover and cook in the oven for 2½ hours or until the beef is meltingly tender. Check halfway through cooking – if the beef looks dry, add the hot beef stock. Serve with the minted soured cream, drizzled with a little olive oil and a grinding of black pepper, and some creamy mashed potatoes and green vegetables.

GET AHEAD
To prepare ahead *Complete the recipe. Cool and chill (it will keep for up to three days) or freeze (it will keep for up to one month).*
To use *If frozen, thaw overnight at a cool room temperature. Return the goulash to the casserole, bring to the boil and simmer gently for 15–20 minutes until piping hot, adding 100ml (3½fl oz) hot beef stock if it looks dry.*

Spicy Pork & Bean Stew

Preparation Time 15 minutes • Cooking Time 50–55 minutes • Serves 4 • Per Serving 348 calories, 14g fat
(of which 3g saturates), 27g carbohydrate, 1.5g salt • Easy

3 tbsp olive oil

400g (14oz) pork escalopes, cut
   into cubes

1 red onion, sliced

2 leeks, trimmed and cut into
   chunks

2 celery sticks, cut into chunks

1 tbsp harissa paste

1 tbsp tomato purée

400g (14oz) cherry tomatoes

300ml (½ pint) hot vegetable or
   chicken stock

400g can cannellini beans, drained
   and rinsed

1 marinated red pepper, sliced

salt and ground black pepper

freshly chopped flat-leafed parsley
   to garnish

Greek yogurt, lemon wedges and
   bread to serve

1. Preheat the oven to 180°C
(160°C fan oven) mark 4. Heat 2
tbsp oil in a flameproof casserole
and fry the pork in batches until
golden. Remove from the pan and
put to one side.

2. Heat the remaining oil in the
pan and fry the onion for 5–10
minutes until softened. Add the
leeks and celery and cook for
about 5 minutes. Return the pork
to the pan, and add the harissa
and tomato purée. Cook for 1–2
minutes, stirring all the time. Add
the tomatoes and hot stock, and
season well with salt and pepper.
Bring to the boil, then transfer to
the oven and cook for 25 minutes.

3. Add the drained beans and red
pepper to the mixture and put
back into the oven for 5 minutes to
warm through. Garnish with
parsley and serve with a dollop of
Greek yogurt, a grinding of black
pepper, lemon wedges for
squeezing over the stew, and
chunks of crusty baguette or
wholegrain bread.

Spiced Lamb with Lentils

Preparation Time 10 minutes • Cooking Time 2 hours • Serves 4 • Per Serving 459 calories, 17g fat (of which 6g saturates), 36g carbohydrate, 1.1g salt • Easy

1 tbsp sunflower oil

8 lamb chops, trimmed of all fat

2 onions, sliced

1 tsp each paprika and ground cinnamon

400g can lentils, drained

400g can chickpeas, drained and rinsed

300ml (½ pint) lamb or chicken stock

salt and ground black pepper

freshly chopped flat-leafed parsley to garnish

1. Preheat the oven to 180°C (160°C fan oven) mark 4. Heat the oil in a large non-stick frying pan, add the chops and brown on both sides. Remove from the pan with a slotted spoon.

2. Add the onions, paprika and cinnamon and fry for 2–3 minutes. Stir in the lentils and chickpeas, and season, then spoon into a shallow 2 litre (3½ pint) ovenproof dish.

3. Put the chops on top of the onion and lentil mixture and pour the stock over them.

4. Cover the dish tightly and cook in the oven for 1½ hours or until the chops are tender. Uncover and cook for 30 minutes or until lightly browned. Serve garnished with parsley.

Lamb, Potato & Peanut Curry

Preparation Time 20 minutes • Cooking Time about 2 hours • Serves 8 • Per Serving 664 calories, 47g fat (of which 20g saturates), 19g carbohydrate, 0.5g salt • Easy

2 tbsp olive oil

1 medium onion, chopped

1 tbsp peeled and grated fresh root ginger

1.6kg (3½lb) leg of lamb, diced

3–4 tbsp Massaman paste (see Cook's Tip)

1 tbsp fish sauce

2 tbsp peanut butter

100g (3½oz) ground almonds

400ml can coconut milk

600ml (1 pint) hot chicken stock

1–2 tbsp dry sherry

500g (1lb 2oz) small potatoes, peeled and quartered

200g (7oz) green beans, trimmed

75g (3oz) toasted peanuts, roughly chopped

20g pack coriander, finely chopped

2 limes, quartered

rice to serve

COOK'S TIP
Massaman paste is a Thai curry paste. The ingredients include red chillies, roasted shallots, roasted garlic, galangal, lemongrass, roasted coriander seeds, roasted cumin, roasted cloves, white pepper, salt and shrimp paste. It's available in supermarkets or Asian food stores.

1. Preheat the oven to 170°C (150°C fan oven) mark 3. Heat the oil in a large flameproof casserole. Add the onion and cook over a medium heat for 7–8 minutes until golden. Add the ginger and cook for 1 minute. Spoon the onion mixture out of the pan and set aside. Add the lamb and fry in batches until browned. Put to one side.

2. Add the Massaman paste, fish sauce and peanut butter to the casserole and fry for 2–3 minutes, then add the reserved onion and ginger mixture, lamb pieces, the ground almonds, coconut milk, hot stock and sherry.

3. Bring to the boil, then cover with a lid and cook in the oven for 1 hour. Add the potatoes and cook for a further 40 minutes, uncovered, adding the green beans for the last 20 minutes. Garnish the curry with toasted peanuts and coriander. Serve with freshly cooked rice and lime wedges to squeeze over the curry.

Salmon Laksa Curry

Preparation Time 10 minutes • Cooking Time about 20 minutes • Serves 4 • Per Serving 570 calories, 22g fat (of which 3g saturates), 55g carbohydrate, 1.9g salt • Easy

1 tbsp olive oil
1 onion, thinly sliced
3 tbsp laksa paste (see Cook's Tip)
200ml (7fl oz) coconut milk
900ml (1½ pints) hot vegetable
   stock
200g (7oz) baby sweetcorn, halved
   lengthways
600g (1lb 5oz) piece skinless
   salmon fillet, cut into
   1cm (½in) slices

225g (8oz) baby leaf spinach
250g (9oz) medium rice noodles
salt and ground black pepper

TO GARNISH
2 spring onions, sliced diagonally
2 tbsp freshly chopped coriander
1 lime, cut into wedges

1. Heat the oil in a wok or large frying pan, then add the onion and fry over a medium heat for 10 minutes, stirring, until golden. Add the laksa paste and cook for 2 minutes.

2. Add the coconut milk, hot stock and sweetcorn, and season with salt and pepper. Bring to the boil, then reduce the heat and simmer for 5 minutes.

3. Add the salmon slices and spinach, stirring to immerse them in the liquid. Cook for 4 minutes or until the fish is opaque all the way through.

4. Meanwhile, put the noodles into a large heatproof bowl, pour boiling water over to cover and soak for 30 seconds. Drain well, then stir them into the curry. Pour the curry into four warmed bowls and garnish with the spring onions and coriander. Serve immediately with lime wedges.

COOK'S TIP
Laksa paste is a hot and spicy paste; you could use Thai curry paste instead.

TRY SOMETHING DIFFERENT
Instead of the medium rice noodles try using rice vermicelli, or leave out the noodles and serve with basmati rice.

Thai Green Shellfish Curry

Preparation Time 10 minutes • Cooking Time 10–15 minutes • Serves 6 • Per Serving 156 calories, 5g fat (of which 1g saturates), 6g carbohydrate, 0.8g salt • Easy

1 tbsp vegetable oil
1 lemongrass stalk, trimmed
    and chopped
2 small red chillies, seeded
    and chopped (see Cook's Tip,
    page 20)
a handful of fresh coriander leaves,
    chopped, plus extra to serve
2 kaffir lime leaves, chopped
1–2 tbsp Thai green curry paste

400ml can coconut milk
450ml (¾ pint) vegetable stock
375g (13oz) queen scallops
    with corals
250g (9oz) raw tiger prawns, peeled
    and deveined (see Cook's Tip,
    page 133), with tails intact
salt and ground black pepper
jasmine rice to serve

1. Heat the oil in a wok or large frying pan. Add the lemongrass, chillies, coriander and lime leaves and stir-fry for 30 seconds. Add the curry paste and fry for 1 minute.

2. Add the coconut milk and stock to the wok or pan, and bring to the boil, then reduce the heat and simmer for 5–10 minutes until slightly reduced. Season well with salt and pepper.

3. Add the scallops and tiger prawns and bring to the boil, then reduce the heat and simmer gently for 2–3 minutes until cooked.

4. Divide the rice among six bowls and spoon the curry on top. Sprinkle with coriander and serve immediately.

TRY SOMETHING DIFFERENT
Use cleaned squid or mussels instead of scallops and prawns.

Prawn Madras with Coconut Chutney

Preparation Time 10 minutes • Cooking Time 25 minutes • Serves 4 • Per Serving 415 calories, 30g fat (of which 18g saturates), 15g carbohydrate, 1.8g salt • A Little Effort

2 tbsp groundnut oil

1 medium onion, finely sliced

1 green chilli, seeded and finely chopped (see Cook's Tip, page 20)

600ml (1 pint) vegetable stock

450g (1lb) raw king prawns, peeled and deveined (see Cook's Tip, page 133)

2 bay leaves

fresh coriander leaves to garnish

basmati rice to serve

FOR THE MADRAS PASTE

1 small onion, finely chopped

2.5cm (1in) piece fresh root ginger, peeled and finely chopped

2 garlic cloves, crushed

juice of ½ lemon

1 tbsp each cumin seeds and coriander seeds

1 tsp cayenne pepper

2 tsp each ground turmeric and garam masala

1 tsp salt

FOR THE COCONUT CHUTNEY

1 tbsp groundnut oil

1 tbsp black mustard seeds

1 medium onion, grated

125g (4oz) desiccated coconut

1 red chilli, seeded and diced (see Cook's Tip, page 20)

1. Put all the ingredients for the Madras paste into a food processor with 2 tbsp water and blend until smooth. Divide the paste into three equal portions, freeze two (see Freezing Tip) and put the other into a large bowl.

2. To make the coconut chutney, heat the oil in a pan and add the mustard seeds. Cover the pan with a lid and cook over a medium heat until the seeds pop – you'll hear them jumping against the lid. Add the grated onion, coconut and red chilli, and cook for 3–4 minutes to toast the coconut. Remove from the heat and put to one side.

3. To make the curry, heat the oil in a pan, add the onion and fry for 10 minutes or until soft and golden.

Add the Madras paste and green chilli, and cook for 5 minutes. Add the stock and bring to the boil. Reduce the heat to a simmer and add the prawns and bay leaves. Cook for 3–5 minutes until the prawns turn pink. Garnish with coriander and serve with the coconut chutney and basmati rice.

FREEZING TIP

At the end of step 1, put two of the portions of Madras paste into separate freezer bags and freeze. They will keep for up to three months.

To use the frozen paste *Put the paste into a microwave and cook on Defrost for 1 minute 20 seconds (based on a 900W oven), or thaw at a cool room temperature for 1 hour.*

Lentil Chilli

Preparation Time 10 minutes • Cooking Time 30 minutes • Serves 6 • Per Serving 195 calories, 2g fat
(of which trace saturates), 32g carbohydrate, 0.1g salt • Vegetarian • Easy

oil-water spray (see Cook's Tip,
   page 35)
2 red onions, chopped
1½ tsp each ground coriander and
   ground cumin
½ tsp ground paprika
2 garlic cloves, crushed
2 sun-dried tomatoes, chopped
¼ tsp dried chilli flakes
125ml (4fl oz) red wine
300ml (½ pint) hot vegetable stock
2 × 400g cans brown or green
   lentils, drained and rinsed
2 × 400g cans chopped tomatoes
sugar to taste
salt and ground black pepper
natural low-fat yogurt and rice
   to serve

1. Spray a saucepan with the oil-water spray and cook the onions for 5 minutes or until softened. Add the ground coriander, cumin and paprika. Combine the crushed garlic, sun-dried tomatoes, chilli, wine and stock, and add to the pan. Cover and simmer for 5–7 minutes. Uncover and simmer until the onions are very tender and the liquid has almost gone.

2. Stir in the lentils and canned tomatoes and season with salt and pepper. Simmer, uncovered, for 15 minutes or until thick. Stir in sugar to taste. Remove from the heat.

3. Ladle out a quarter of the mixture and whiz in a food processor or blender. Combine the puréed and unpuréed portions. Serve with yogurt and rice.

Black-eyed Bean Chilli

Preparation Time 10 minutes • Cooking Time 20 minutes • Serves 4 • Per Serving 245 calories, 5g fat (of which 1g saturates), 39g carbohydrate, 1.8g salt • Vegetarian • Easy

- 1 tbsp olive oil
- 1 onion, chopped
- 3 celery sticks, finely chopped
- 2 × 400g cans black-eyed beans, drained and rinsed
- 2 × 400g cans chopped tomatoes
- 2 or 3 splashes of Tabasco sauce
- 3 tbsp freshly chopped coriander
- 4 warmed tortillas and soured cream to serve

1. Heat the oil in a frying pan. Add the onion and celery, and cook for 10 minutes until softened.

2. Add the beans, tomatoes and Tabasco to the pan. Bring to the boil, then reduce the heat and simmer for 10 minutes.

3. Just before serving, stir in the coriander. Spoon the chilli on to the warm tortillas, roll up and serve with soured cream.

TRY SOMETHING DIFFERENT
Replace half the black-eye beans with red kidney beans.

Spicy Bean & Tomato Fajitas

Preparation Time 15 minutes • Cooking Time 25 minutes • Serves 6 • Per Serving 512 calories, 20g fat (of which 6g saturates), 71g carbohydrate, 1.5g salt • Vegetarian • Easy

2 tbsp sunflower oil

1 onion, sliced

2 garlic cloves, crushed

½ tsp hot chilli powder, plus extra to garnish

1 tsp each ground coriander and ground cumin

1 tbsp tomato purée

400g can chopped tomatoes

200g can red kidney beans, drained and rinsed

400g can borlotti beans, drained and rinsed

400g can flageolet beans, drained and rinsed

150ml (¼ pint) hot vegetable stock

2 ripe avocados

juice of ½ lime

1 tbsp freshly chopped coriander, plus sprigs to garnish

6 ready-made flour tortillas

150ml (¼ pint) soured cream

salt and ground black pepper

lime wedges to serve

1. Heat the oil in a large pan, add the onion and cook gently for 5 minutes. Add the garlic and spices and cook for a further 2 minutes.

2. Add the tomato purée and cook for 1 minute, then add the tomatoes, beans and hot stock. Season well with salt and pepper and bring to the boil, then reduce the heat and simmer for 15 minutes, stirring occasionally.

3. Halve, stone and peel the avocados, then chop. Put the avocado into a bowl, add the lime juice and chopped coriander, and mash. Season to taste.

4. Warm the tortillas: either wrap them in foil and heat in the oven at 180°C (160°C fan oven) mark 4 for 10 minutes, or put on to a plate and microwave on full power for 45 seconds (based on a 900W oven).

5. Spoon some beans down the centre of each tortilla. Fold up the bottom to keep the filling inside, then wrap the sides in so that they overlap. Spoon on the avocado and soured cream. Sprinkle with chilli powder and coriander sprigs and serve with lime wedges.

Curried Coconut & Vegetable Rice

Preparation Time 15 minutes • Cooking Time 30 minutes, plus standing • Serves 6 • Per Serving 413 calories, 17g fat (of which 2g saturates), 57g carbohydrate, 0.4g salt • Vegetarian • Easy

1 large aubergine, about 300g (11oz), trimmed
1 large butternut squash, about 500g (1lb 2oz), peeled and seeded
250g (9oz) dwarf green beans, trimmed
100ml (3½fl oz) vegetable oil
1 large onion, chopped
1 tbsp black mustard seeds
3 tbsp korma paste
350g (12oz) basmati rice
400ml can coconut milk
200g (7oz) baby spinach leaves
salt and ground black pepper

1. Cut the aubergine and butternut squash into 2cm (¾in) cubes. Slice the beans into 2cm (¾in) pieces.

2. Heat the oil in a large pan. Add the onion and cook for about 5 minutes or until a light golden colour. Add the mustard seeds and cook, stirring, until they begin to pop. Stir in the korma paste and cook for 1 minute.

3. Add the aubergine and cook, stirring, for 5 minutes. Add the butternut squash, beans, rice and 2 tsp salt, mixing well. Pour in the coconut milk and add 600ml (1 pint) water. Bring to the boil, cover and simmer for 15–18 minutes.

4. When the rice and vegetables are cooked, remove the lid and put the spinach leaves on top. Cover and leave, off the heat, for 5 minutes. Gently stir the wilted spinach through the rice, check the seasoning and serve immediately.

Chilli Bean Cake

Preparation Time 10 minutes • Cooking Time 20 minutes • Serves 4 • Per Serving 265 calories, 6g fat (of which 1g saturates), 41g carbohydrate, 2.1g salt • Vegetarian • Easy

3 tbsp olive oil

75g (3oz) wholemeal breadcrumbs

1 bunch of spring onions, finely chopped

1 orange pepper, seeded and chopped

1 small green chilli, seeded and finely chopped (see Cook's Tip, page 20)

1 garlic clove, crushed

1 tsp ground turmeric (optional)

400g can mixed beans, drained and rinsed

3 tbsp mayonnaise

a small handful of fresh basil, chopped

salt and ground black pepper

TO SERVE

soured cream

freshly chopped coriander

lime wedges (optional)

1. Heat 2 tbsp oil in a non-stick frying pan over a medium heat and fry the breadcrumbs until golden and beginning to crisp. Remove and put to one side.

2. Add the remaining oil to the pan and fry the spring onions until soft and golden. Add the orange pepper, chilli, garlic and turmeric, if using. Cook, stirring, for 5 minutes.

3. Tip in the beans, mayonnaise, two-thirds of the fried breadcrumbs and the basil. Season with salt and pepper, mash roughly with a fork, then press the mixture down to flatten and sprinkle with the remaining breadcrumbs. Fry the bean cake over a medium heat for 4–5 minutes until the base is golden. Remove from the heat, cut into wedges and serve with soured cream, coriander and the lime wedges, if you like.

Spiced Egg Pilau

Preparation Time 5 minutes • Cooking Time 15 minutes • Serves 4 • Per Serving 331 calories, 9g fat (of which 12g saturates), 50g carbohydrate, 0.6g salt • Vegetarian • Easy

200g (7oz) basmati or wild rice

150g (5oz) frozen peas

4 medium eggs

200ml (7fl oz) coconut cream

1 tsp mild curry paste (see Cook's Tip, page 21)

1 tbsp sweet chilli sauce

1 tbsp smooth peanut butter

1 large bunch of fresh coriander, roughly chopped

mini poppadums and mango chutney to serve

1. Put the rice into a pan with 450ml (¾ pint) boiling water over a low heat and cook for 15 minutes or until just tender. Add the peas for the last 5 minutes of cooking time.

2. Meanwhile, put the eggs into a large pan of boiling water, then reduce the heat and simmer for 6 minutes. Drain and shell.

3. Put the coconut cream, curry paste, chilli sauce and peanut butter into a small pan and whisk together. Heat the sauce gently, stirring, without allowing it to boil.

4. Drain the rice and stir in the chopped coriander and 2 tbsp of the sauce.

5. Divide the rice among four bowls. Cut the eggs into halves and serve on the rice, spooning the remaining coconut sauce over the top. Serve with poppadums and chutney.

Chickpea & Chilli Stir-fry

Preparation Time 10 minutes • Cooking Time 15–20 minutes • Serves 4 • Per Serving 258 calories, 11g fat (of which 1g saturates), 30g carbohydrate, 1g salt • Vegetarian • Easy

2 tbsp olive oil

1 tsp ground cumin

1 red onion, sliced

2 garlic cloves, finely chopped

1 red chilli, seeded and finely chopped (see **Cook's Tip, page 20**)

2 × 400g cans chickpeas, drained and rinsed

400g (14oz) cherry tomatoes

125g (4oz) baby spinach leaves

salt and ground black pepper

brown rice or pasta to serve

1. Heat the oil in a wok or large frying pan. Add the cumin and fry for 1–2 minutes. Add the onion and stir-fry for 5–7 minutes.

2. Add the garlic and chilli, and stir-fry for 2 minutes.

3. Add the chickpeas to the wok with the tomatoes. Reduce the heat and simmer until the chickpeas are hot. Season with salt and pepper. Add the spinach and cook for 1–2 minutes until the leaves have wilted. Serve with brown rice or pasta.

Tofu Noodle Curry

Preparation Time 15 minutes, plus marinating • Cooking Time about 25 minutes • Serves 4 • Per Serving
367 calories, 7g fat (of which 1g saturates), 60g carbohydrate, 2g salt • Vegetarian • Easy

250g (9oz) fresh tofu
2 tbsp light soy sauce
½ red chilli, chopped (see Cook's Tip, page 20)
5cm (2in) piece fresh root ginger, peeled and grated
1 tbsp olive oil
1 onion, finely sliced
2 tbsp Thai red curry paste (see Cook's Tip)
200ml (7fl oz) coconut milk

900ml (1½ pints) hot vegetable stock
200g (7oz) baby sweetcorn, halved lengthways
200g (7oz) fine green beans
250g (9oz) medium rice noodles
salt and ground black pepper
2 spring onions, sliced diagonally, and 2 tbsp fresh coriander leaves to garnish
1 lime, cut into wedges, to serve

1. Drain the tofu, pat it dry and cut it into large cubes. Put the tofu into a shallow dish with the soy sauce, chilli and ginger. Toss to coat, then leave to marinate for 30 minutes.

2. Heat the oil in a large pan over a medium heat, then add the onion and fry for 10 minutes, stirring, until golden. Add the curry paste and cook for 2 minutes.

3. Add the tofu and marinade, coconut milk, hot stock and sweetcorn, and season with salt and pepper. Bring to the boil, add the green beans, then reduce the heat and simmer for 8–10 minutes.

4. Meanwhile, put the noodles into a large bowl, pour boiling water over them and soak for 30 seconds. Drain the noodles, then stir into the curry. Pour into bowls and garnish with the spring onions and coriander. Serve immediately, with lime wedges.

COOK'S TIP
Check the ingredients in the Thai curry paste: some contain shrimp and are therefore not suitable for vegetarians.

Thai Vegetable Curry

Preparation Time 10 minutes • Cooking Time 15 minutes • Serves 4 • Per Serving 200 calories, 10g fat
(of which 2g saturates), 19g carbohydrate, 0.7g salt • Vegetarian • Easy

2–3 tbsp red Thai curry paste (see Cook's Tip, page 21)
2.5cm (1in) piece fresh root ginger, peeled and finely chopped
50g (2oz) cashew nuts
400ml can coconut milk
3 carrots, cut into thin batons
1 broccoli head, cut into florets
20g (¾oz) fresh coriander, roughly chopped
zest and juice of 1 lime
2 large handfuls of spinach leaves
basmati rice to serve

1. Put the curry paste into a large pan, add the ginger and cashew nuts and stir-fry over a medium heat for 2–3 minutes.

2. Add the coconut milk, cover and bring to the boil. Stir the carrots into the pan, then reduce the heat and simmer for 5 minutes. Add the broccoli florets and simmer for a further 5 minutes until tender.

3. Stir the coriander and lime zest into the pan with the spinach. Squeeze the lime juice over and serve with basmati rice.

TRY SOMETHING DIFFERENT
Replace the carrots and/or broccoli with alternative vegetables – try baby sweetcorn, sugarsnap peas or mangetouts and simmer for only 5 minutes until tender.

Chickpea Curry

Preparation Time 20 minutes • Cooking Time 40–45 minutes • Serves 6 • Per Serving 291 calories, 8g fat (of which 1g saturates), 46g carbohydrate, 1.3g salt • Vegetarian • Easy

2 tbsp vegetable oil

2 onions, finely sliced

2 garlic cloves, crushed

1 tbsp ground coriander

1 tsp mild chilli powder

1 tbsp black mustard seeds

2 tbsp tamarind paste

2 tbsp sun-dried tomato paste

750g (1lb 10oz) new potatoes, quartered

400g can chopped tomatoes

1 litre (1¾ pints) hot vegetable stock

250g (9oz) green beans, trimmed

2 × 400g cans chickpeas, drained and rinsed

2 tsp garam masala

salt and ground black pepper

1. Heat the oil in a pan and fry the onions for 10–15 minutes until golden – when they have a good colour they will add depth of flavour. Add the garlic, coriander, chilli, mustard seeds, tamarind paste and sun-dried tomato paste. Cook for 1–2 minutes until the aroma from the spices is released.

2. Add the potatoes and toss in the spices for 1–2 minutes. Add the tomatoes and hot stock and season with salt and pepper. Cover and bring to the boil, then reduce the heat and simmer, half covered, for 20 minutes or until the potatoes are just cooked.

3. Add the beans and chickpeas, and continue to cook for 5 minutes or until the beans are tender and the chickpeas are warmed through. Stir in the garam masala and serve.

COOK'S TIP
Tamarind paste has a very sharp, sour flavour and is widely used in Asian and South-east Asian cooking.

Aubergine & Pepper Balti with Carrot Relish

Preparation Time 30 minutes • Cooking Time 45 minutes • Serves 4 • Per Serving 364 calories, 18g fat (of which 2g saturates), 47g carbohydrate, 0.4g salt • Vegetarian • Easy

4 tbsp groundnut oil, plus 1 tsp
   for the relish
1 onion, finely sliced
1 aubergine, cut into 2cm
   (¾in) dice
1 red and 1 green chilli, seeded and
   roughly chopped (see Cook's Tip,
   page 20)
1 red and 1 green pepper, seeded
   and sliced
4 tomatoes, about 300g (11oz),
   quartered
600ml (1 pint) vegetable stock
2 tsp black mustard seeds
450g (1lb) carrots, peeled
   and grated
2 tbsp tamarind paste (see Cook's
   Tip, page 169)
2 tbsp dark muscovado sugar
1 tbsp white wine vinegar
50g (2oz) baby spinach leaves
salt and ground black pepper
pilau rice to serve

FOR THE BALTI PASTE

1 tbsp each fennel seeds and
   ground allspice
2–3 garlic cloves, roughly chopped
1cm (½in) piece fresh root ginger,
   peeled and roughly chopped
50g (2oz) garam masala
25g (1oz) curry powder
1 tsp salt

1. Put all the ingredients for the balti paste into a food processor with 8 tbsp water and blend. Divide the paste into three equal portions, freeze two (see Freezing Tip, page 156) and put the other to one side.

2. To make the curry, heat 4 tbsp oil in a large flameproof casserole and fry the onion over a high heat for 10–15 minutes until golden. Add the aubergine and cook for another 5 minutes.

3. Add the balti paste and the chillies to the casserole, stir well to mix and cook for 1–2 minutes. Add the peppers and tomatoes, and cook for 5 minutes, then add the stock and season well. Cover and bring to the boil, then reduce the heat and simmer the balti for 15 minutes or until the vegetables are tender.

4. Meanwhile, make the carrot relish. Heat the 1 tsp oil in a pan and add the mustard seeds. Cover with a lid and cook until they start to pop – you'll hear them jumping against the lid. Add the carrots, tamarind paste, sugar and vinegar to the pan and cook for 1–2 minutes. Stir well.

5. Stir the spinach into the curry and serve with the carrot relish and pilau rice to soak up the sauce.

Veggie Curry

Preparation Time 5 minutes • Cooking Time 12 minutes • Serves 1 • Per Serving 468 calories, 20g fat of which 3g saturates), 58g carbohydrate, 1.4g salt • Vegetarian • Easy

1 tbsp medium curry paste (see Cook's Tip, page 21)
227g can chopped tomatoes
150ml (¼ pint) hot vegetable stock
200g (7oz) vegetables, such as broccoli, courgettes and sugarsnap peas, roughly chopped
½ × 400g can chickpeas, drained and rinsed
griddled wholemeal pitta bread and yogurt to serve

1. Heat the curry paste in a large heavy-based pan for 1 minute, stirring the paste to warm the spices. Add the tomatoes and hot stock. Bring to the boil, then reduce the heat to a simmer and add the vegetables. Simmer for 5–6 minutes until the vegetables are tender.

2. Stir in the chickpeas and heat for 1–2 minutes until hot. Serve the vegetable curry with a griddled wholemeal pitta and yogurt.

Mauritian Vegetable Curry

Preparation Time 15 minutes • Cooking Time 30 minutes • Serves 4 • Per Serving 184 calories, 11g fat (of which 1g saturates), 18g carbohydrate, 1.7g salt • Vegetarian • Easy

3 tbsp vegetable oil

1 onion, finely sliced

4 garlic cloves, crushed

2.5cm (1in) piece fresh root ginger, peeled and grated

3 tbsp medium curry powder

6 fresh curry leaves

150g (5oz) potato, cut into 1cm (½in) cubes

125g (4oz) aubergine, cut into 2cm (¾in) sticks, 5mm (¼in) wide

150g (5oz) carrots, cut into 5mm (¼in) dice

900ml (1½ pints) hot vegetable stock

a pinch of saffron

1 tsp salt

150g (5oz) green beans, trimmed

75g (3oz) frozen peas

ground black pepper

3 tbsp freshly chopped coriander to garnish

pitta bread to serve

1. Heat the oil in a large heavy-based pan over a low heat. Add the onion and fry for 5–10 minutes until golden. Add the garlic, ginger, curry powder and curry leaves, and fry for a further minute.

2. Add the potato and aubergine to the pan and fry, stirring, for 2 minutes. Add the carrots, hot stock, saffron and salt, and season with plenty of pepper. Cover and cook for 10 minutes or until the vegetables are almost tender.

3. Add the beans and peas to the pan and cook for a further 4 minutes. Sprinkle with the chopped coriander and serve with pitta bread.

GET AHEAD

To prepare ahead *Complete the recipe, without the garnish, and chill quickly. It will keep, in the fridge, for up to two days.*
To use *Put into a pan, cover and bring to the boil, then simmer for 10–15 minutes. Complete the recipe.*

VEGETABLE DISHES

Leek & Broccoli Bake

Preparation Time 20 minutes • Cooking Time 45–55 minutes • Serves 4 • Per Serving 245 calories, 13g fat (of which 4g saturates), 18g carbohydrate, 0.4g salt • Vegetarian • Easy

2 tbsp olive oil
1 large red onion, cut into wedges
1 aubergine, chopped
2 leeks, trimmed and cut
   into chunks
1 broccoli head, cut into florets
   and stalks chopped
3 large flat mushrooms, chopped
2 × 400g cans cherry tomatoes
3 rosemary sprigs, chopped
50g (2oz) Parmesan, freshly grated
   (see Cook's Tips, page 177)
salt and ground black pepper

1. Preheat the oven to 200°C (180°C fan oven) mark 6. Heat the oil in a large flameproof dish, add the onion, aubergine and leeks, and cook for 10–12 minutes until golden and softened.

2. Add the broccoli, mushrooms, cherry tomatoes, half the rosemary and 300ml (½ pint) boiling water. Season with salt and pepper. Stir well, then cover and cook in the oven for 30 minutes.

3. Meanwhile, put the Parmesan into a bowl. Add the remaining rosemary and season with pepper. When the vegetables are cooked, remove the lid and sprinkle the Parmesan mixture on top. Cook, uncovered, in the oven for a further 5–10 minutes until the topping is golden.

TRY SOMETHING DIFFERENT
Use sliced courgettes instead of aubergine.

Cheese & Vegetable Bake

Preparation Time 15 minutes • Cooking Time 15 minutes • Serves 4 • Per Serving 471 calories, 13g fat (of which 7g saturates), 67g carbohydrate, 0.8g salt • Vegetarian • Easy

250g (9oz) macaroni

1 cauliflower, cut into florets

2 leeks, trimmed and finely chopped

100g (3½oz) frozen peas

25g (1oz) wholemeal breadcrumbs

crusty bread to serve

FOR THE CHEESE SAUCE

15g (½oz) butter

15g (½oz) plain flour

200ml (7fl oz) skimmed milk

75g (3oz) Parmesan, grated (see Cook's Tips)

2 tsp Dijon mustard

salt and ground black pepper

1. Cook the macaroni in a large pan of boiling water for 6 minutes, adding the cauliflower and leeks for the last 4 minutes and the peas for the last 2 minutes.

2. Meanwhile, make the cheese sauce. Melt the butter in a pan and add the flour. Cook for 1–2 minutes, then take off the heat and gradually stir in the milk. Bring to the boil slowly, stirring until the sauce thickens. Stir in 50g (2oz) Parmesan and the mustard. Season with salt and pepper.

3. Preheat the grill to medium. Drain the pasta and vegetables and put back into the pan. Add the cheese sauce and mix well. Spoon into a large shallow 2 litre (3½ pint) ovenproof dish and scatter the remaining Parmesan and the breadcrumbs over the top. Grill for 5 minutes or until golden and crisp. Serve hot with bread.

COOK'S TIPS

Microwave Cheese Sauce
Put the butter, flour and milk into a large microwave-proof bowl and whisk together. Cook in a 900W microwave oven on full power for 4 minutes, whisking every minute, until the sauce has thickened. Stir in the cheese until it melts. Stir in the mustard and season to taste.

Vegetarian cheeses *Some vegetarians prefer to avoid cheeses that have been produced by the traditional method, because this uses animal-derived rennet. Most supermarkets and cheese shops now stock an excellent range of vegetarian cheeses, produced using vegetarian rennet, which comes from plants, such as thistle and mallow, that contain enzymes capable of curdling milk.*

Mushroom & Roasted Potato Bake

Preparation Time 15 minutes • Cooking Time 1¼ hours • Serves 6 • Per Serving 809 calories, 63g fat (of which 31g saturates), 33g carbohydrate, 1.7g salt • Vegetarian • Easy

900g (2lb) small potatoes, quartered
6 tbsp olive oil
225g (8oz) onions, roughly chopped
450g (1lb) mixed fresh mushrooms, such as shiitake and brown-cap, roughly chopped
2 garlic cloves, crushed
2 tbsp tomato purée
4 tbsp sun-dried tomato paste
25g (1oz) dried porcini mushrooms, rinsed (optional)

2 tsp freshly chopped thyme
300ml (½ pint) each of dry white wine and vegetable stock
300ml (½ pint) double cream
400g (14oz) large fresh spinach leaves, roughly chopped
175g (6oz) Gruyère cheese
125g (4oz) freshly grated Parmesan (see Cook's Tips, page 177)
300g (11oz) Greek yogurt
2 medium eggs, beaten
salt and ground black pepper

1. Preheat the oven to 200°C (180°C fan oven) mark 6. Toss the potatoes with 4 tbsp oil in a roasting tin and cook in the oven for 40 minutes or until tender.

2. Heat the remaining oil in a large heavy-based pan. Add the onions and cook for 10 minutes or until soft, then add the fresh mushrooms and garlic, and cook over a high heat for 5 minutes. Stir in the tomato purée and tomato paste, the porcini mushrooms, if using, and the thyme and wine. Bring to the boil and simmer for 2 minutes. Add the stock and cream and bring to the boil, then bubble for 20 minutes or until well reduced and syrupy.

3. Pour into a 2.4 litre (4¼ pint) ovenproof dish. Stir in the potatoes, spinach, Gruyère and half the Parmesan. Season well with salt and pepper.

4. Combine the yogurt with the eggs and season. Spoon over the vegetable mixture and sprinkle with the remaining Parmesan. Cook in the oven for 30–35 minutes until golden and bubbling. Serve hot.

FREEZING TIP

To freeze Complete the recipe to the end of step 4, then cool and freeze for up to one month.
To use Thaw overnight at cool room temperature. Preheat the oven to 200°C (180°C fan oven) mark 6. Bake for 40–45 minutes until golden and bubbling.

Baked Stuffed Pumpkin

Preparation Time about 40 minutes • Cooking Time 1½ hours–1 hour 50 minutes, plus standing • Serves 4 •
Per Serving 438 calories, 24g fat (of which 9g saturates), 38g carbohydrate, 0.7g salt • Vegetarian • Easy

1 pumpkin, about 1.4–1.8kg (3–4lb)
2 tbsp olive oil
2 leeks, trimmed and chopped
2 garlic cloves, crushed
2 tbsp freshly chopped thyme
   leaves
2 tsp paprika
1 tsp turmeric
125g (4oz) long-grain rice, cooked
2 tomatoes, peeled, seeded and
   diced
50g (2oz) cashew nuts, toasted and
   roughly chopped

125g (4oz) vegetarian Cheddar
   cheese, grated
salt and ground black pepper

1. Cut a 5cm (2in) slice from the top of the pumpkin and put to one side for the lid. Scoop out and discard the seeds. Using a knife and a spoon, cut out most of the pumpkin flesh, leaving a thin shell. Cut the pumpkin flesh into small pieces and put to one side.

2. Heat the oil in a large pan, add the leeks, garlic, thyme, paprika and turmeric and fry for 10 minutes. Add the chopped pumpkin flesh and fry for a further 10 minutes or until golden, stirring frequently to prevent sticking. Transfer the mixture to a bowl. Preheat the oven to 180°C (160°C fan oven) mark 4.

3. Add the pumpkin mixture to the cooked rice along with the tomatoes, cashew nuts and cheese. Fork through to mix and season with salt and pepper.

4. Spoon the stuffing mixture into the pumpkin shell, top with the lid and bake for 1¼–1½ hours until the pumpkin is softened and the skin is browned. Remove from the oven and leave to stand for 10 minutes. Cut into wedges to serve.

Aubergine Parmigiana

Preparation Time 5 minutes • Cooking Time about 25 minutes • Serves 4 • Per Serving 370 calories, 25g fat (of which 11g saturates), 17g carbohydrate, 2.1g salt • Vegetarian • Easy

2 large aubergines, thinly sliced lengthways

2 tbsp olive oil, plus extra to brush

3 fat garlic cloves, sliced

2 × 200ml tubs fresh napoletana sauce

4 ready-roasted red peppers, roughly chopped

20g (¾oz) fresh basil, roughly chopped (see Cook's Tip)

150g (5oz) Taleggio or Fontina cheese, coarsely grated

50g (2oz) Parmesan, coarsely grated (see Cook's Tips, page 177)

salt and ground black pepper

1. Preheat the oven to 200°C (180°C fan oven) mark 6 and preheat the grill until hot. Put the aubergine on an oiled baking sheet, brush the aubergine with oil, scatter the garlic over and season with salt and pepper. Grill for 5–6 minutes until golden.

2. Spread a little napoletana sauce over the bottom of an oiled ovenproof dish, then cover with a layer of aubergine and peppers, packing the layers together as tightly as you can. Sprinkle a little basil and some of each cheese over the top. Repeat the layers, finishing with a layer of cheese. Season with pepper. Cook in the oven for 20 minutes or until golden. Serve hot.

COOK'S TIP

Choose bags or bunches of fresh basil, as the larger leaves have a stronger, more peppery flavour than those of plants sold in pots.

Vegetable Moussaka

Preparation Time 45 minutes • Cooking Time 1½ hours • Serves 6 • Per Serving 399 calories, 24g fat (of which 11g saturates), 29g carbohydrate, 1.2g salt • Vegetarian • Easy

450g (1lb) potatoes, cut lengthways into 5mm (¼in) slices
1 aubergine, sliced into rounds
1 large red onion, cut into wedges
2 red peppers, seeded and sliced
4 tbsp olive oil
2 tbsp chopped thyme
225g (8oz) tomatoes, thickly sliced
2 garlic cloves, sliced
250g (9oz) passata
250g (9oz) soft goat's cheese
300g (11oz) natural yogurt
3 medium eggs
25g (1oz) freshly grated Parmesan (see Cook's Tips, page 177)
salt and ground black pepper

1. Preheat the oven to 230°C (210°C fan oven) mark 8. Boil the potatoes in a pan of lightly salted water for 5 minutes. Drain and put into a large roasting tin with the aubergine, onion and peppers. Drizzle with oil, add the thyme, toss and season with salt and pepper. Roast for 30 minutes, stirring occasionally.

2. Add the tomatoes and garlic and roast for 15 minutes, then take out of the oven. Reduce the oven temperature to 200°C (180°C fan oven) mark 6.

3. Put half the vegetables into a 1.7 litre (3 pint) ovenproof dish, then spoon half the passata over them and spread the goat's cheese on top. Repeat with the rest of the vegetables and passata. Mix the yogurt with the eggs and Parmesan. Season and then pour over the top of the goat's cheese. Cook in the oven for 45 minutes or until heated through

TRY SOMETHING DIFFERENT
Use sliced sweet potatoes, or butternut squash, seeded and cut into chunks, instead of the potatoes.

Chickpea & Butternut Pot

Preparation Time 10 minutes • Cooking Time 15–20 minutes • Serves 4 • Per Serving 307 calories, 14g fat
(of which 2g saturates), 34g carbohydrate, 2.8g salt • Vegetarian • Easy

**1 large butternut squash, peeled,
   seeded and chopped**
2 tbsp smooth peanut butter
**900ml (1½ pints) hot vegetable
   stock**
2 tbsp olive oil
2 large onions, finely chopped
**1 small red chilli, seeded and
   finely chopped (see Cook's Tips,
   page 20)**
**2 tsp mild curry paste (see Cook's
   Tip, page 21)**
225g (8oz) baby sweetcorn
**2 × 400g cans chickpeas, drained
   and rinsed**
**a handful of freshly chopped
   coriander**
salt and ground black pepper

1. Put the butternut squash, peanut butter and hot stock in a large pan and simmer for 10 minutes until the squash is tender. Remove three-quarters of the squash with a slotted spoon and put to one side. Mash the remaining squash into the liquid, then put the reserved squash back into the pan.

2. Meanwhile, heat the oil in a pan over a low heat and fry the onions, chilli, curry paste and sweetcorn until the onions are soft and caramelised, then tip the contents of the pan into the squash.

3. Add the chickpeas and coriander to the squash and stir through. Season with salt and pepper and cook for 4–5 minutes until piping hot. Serve immediately.

Spiced Bean & Vegetable Stew

Preparation Time 5 minutes • Cooking Time about 30 minutes • Serves 6 • Per Serving 262 calories, 7g fat
(of which 1g saturates), 44g carbohydrate, 1.3g salt • Vegetarian • Easy

3 tbsp olive oil

2 small onions, sliced

2 garlic cloves, crushed

1 tbsp sweet paprika

1 small dried red chilli, seeded
and finely chopped (see Cook's
Tip, page 20)

700g (1½lb) sweet potatoes,
peeled and cubed

700g (1½lb) pumpkin, peeled
and cut into chunks

125g (4oz) okra, trimmed

500g (1lb 2oz) passata

400g can haricot or cannellini
beans, drained and rinsed

salt and ground black pepper

1. Heat the oil in a large heavy pan over a very gentle heat. Add the onion and garlic and cook for 5 minutes. Stir in the paprika and chilli and cook for a further 2 minutes.

2. Add the sweet potatoes, pumpkin, okra, passata and 900ml (1½ pints) water, and season generously with salt and pepper. Cover and bring to the boil, then reduce the heat and simmer for 20 minutes or until the vegetables are tender.

3. Add the haricot or cannellini beans and cook for 3 minutes to warm through. Serve immediately.

COOK'S TIP

Okra contains a mucilaginous juice that can be used as a thickener for stews, but in this dish the okra is used whole in a light sauce. To avoid the juice leaking out, trim off the very tip of the stalk only, so that you don't cut into the pod itself.

Moroccan Chickpea Stew

Preparation Time 10 minutes • Cooking Time 40 minutes • Serves 4 • Per Serving 232 calories, 9g fat (of which 1g saturates), 29g carbohydrate, 0.6g salt • Vegetarian • Easy

1 red pepper, halved and seeded
1 green pepper, halved and seeded
1 yellow pepper, halved and seeded
2 tbsp olive oil
1 onion, finely sliced
2 garlic cloves, crushed
1 tbsp harissa paste
2 tbsp tomato purée
½ tsp ground cumin
1 aubergine, diced
400g can chickpeas, drained
   and rinsed
450ml (¾ pint) vegetable stock
4 tbsp roughly chopped fresh flat-
   leafed parsley, plus a few sprigs
   to garnish
salt and ground black pepper

1. Preheat the grill and lay the peppers, skin side up, on a baking sheet. Grill for about 5 minutes until the skin begins to blister and char. Put the peppers into a plastic bag, seal and put to one side for a few minutes. When cooled a little, peel off the skins and discard, then slice the peppers and put to one side.

2. Heat the oil in a large heavy-based frying pan over a low heat, add the onion and cook for 5–10 minutes until soft. Add the garlic, harissa, tomato purée and cumin, and cook for 2 minutes.

3. Add the peppers to the pan with the aubergine. Stir everything to coat evenly with the spices and cook for 2 minutes. Add the chickpeas and stock, season well with salt and pepper, and bring to the boil. Reduce the heat and simmer for 20 minutes.

4. Just before serving, stir the parsley through the chickpea stew. Serve in warmed bowls, garnished with parsley sprigs.

Mushroom & Bean Hotpot

Preparation Time 15 minutes • Cooking Time 30 minutes • Serves 6 • Per Serving 280 calories, 10g fat (of which 1g saturates), 34g carbohydrate, 1.3g salt • Vegetarian • Easy

3 tbsp olive oil

700g (1½lb) chestnut mushrooms, roughly chopped

1 large onion, finely chopped

2 tbsp plain flour

2 tbsp mild curry paste (see Cook's Tip, page 21)

150ml (¼ pint) dry white wine

400g can chopped tomatoes

2 tbsp sun-dried tomato paste

2 × 400g cans mixed beans, drained and rinsed

3 tbsp mango chutney

3 tbsp roughly chopped fresh coriander and mint

1. Heat the oil in a large pan over a low heat, then fry the mushrooms and onion until the onion is soft and dark golden. Stir in the flour and curry paste and cook for 1–2 minutes.

2. Add the wine, tomatoes, sun-dried tomato paste and beans, and bring to the boil, then reduce the heat and simmer gently for 30 minutes or until most of the liquid has reduced. Stir in the chutney and herbs before serving.

Tomato & Butter Bean Stew

Preparation Time 10 minutes • Cooking Time 50–55 minutes • Serves 4 • Per Serving 286 calories, 8g fat
(of which 1g saturates), 41g carbohydrate, 1.8g salt • Vegetarian • Easy

2 tbsp olive oil

1 onion, finely sliced

2 garlic cloves, finely chopped

2 large leeks, sliced

2 × 400g cans cherry tomatoes

**2 × 400g cans butter beans, drained
   and rinsed**

150ml (¼ pint) hot vegetable stock

1–2 tbsp balsamic vinegar

salt and ground black pepper

1. Preheat the oven to 180°C (160°C fan oven) mark 4. Heat the oil in a flameproof casserole over a medium heat. Add the onion and garlic, and cook for 10 minutes until golden and soft. Add the leeks and cook, covered, for 5 minutes.

2. Add the tomatoes, beans and hot stock, and season well with salt and pepper. Bring to the boil, then cover with a lid and cook in the oven for 35–40 minutes until the sauce has thickened. Remove from the oven, stir in the vinegar and spoon into warmed bowls.

Italian Bean Stew

Preparation time 15 minutes • Cooking time 15 minutes • Serves 4 • Per serving 405 calories, 10g fat
(of which 1g saturates), 35g carbohydrate, 1.3g salt • Easy

1 tbsp olive oil
2 large shallots, finely sliced
2 medium carrots, finely diced
1 celery stick, finely diced
1.5 litres (2 pints 12fl oz) hot
  vegetable stock
250g (9oz) asparagus, cut into
  2cm (¾in) lengths
75g (3oz) tiny soup pasta, such
  as ditalini or stellete
2 × 400g cans flageolet beans,
  drained and rinsed
2 tbsp fresh Pesto to serve
 (see Cook's Tip, page 23)

1. Heat the oil in a large pan. Add the shallots and fry gently for 3 minutes or until softened but not coloured.

2. Add the carrots, celery and hot stock, and bring to the boil. Turn the heat down and simmer for 10 minutes. Add the asparagus and pasta and cook for a further 7 minutes.

3. Stir in the flageolet beans and heat for 2–3 minutes. Divide among the bowls and serve with a swirl of Pesto on top.

Roasted Stuffed Peppers

Preparation Time 20 minutes • Cooking Time 45 minutes • Serves 8 • Per Serving 189 calories, 14g fat
(of which 6g saturates), 11g carbohydrate, 0.9g salt • Vegetarian • Easy

40g (1½oz) butter
4 Romano peppers, halved, with
**   stalks on and seeded**
3 tbsp olive oil
350g (12oz) chestnut mushrooms,
**   roughly chopped**
4 tbsp finely chopped fresh chives
100g (3½oz) vegetarian feta cheese
50g (2oz) fresh white breadcrumbs
25g (1oz) freshly grated Parmesan
**   (see Cook's Tips, page 177)**
salt and ground black pepper

1. Preheat the oven to 180°C (160°C fan oven) mark 4. Use a little butter to grease a shallow ovenproof dish and put the peppers in it side by side, ready to be filled.

2. Heat the remaining butter and 1 tbsp oil in a pan. Add the mushrooms and fry until they're golden and there's no excess liquid left in the pan. Stir in the chives, then spoon the mixture into the pepper halves.

3. Crumble the feta over the mushrooms. Mix the breadcrumbs and Parmesan in a bowl, then sprinkle over the peppers.

4. Season with salt and pepper, and drizzle with the remaining oil. Roast in the oven for 45 minutes or until golden and tender. Serve warm.

GET AHEAD
To prepare ahead Complete the recipe to the end of step 4, up to one day ahead. Cover and chill.
To use Reheat under the grill for 5 minutes.

Spicy Beans with Jazzed-up Potatoes

Preparation Time 12 minutes • Cooking Time about 1½ hours • Serves 4 • Per Serving 298 calories, 4g fat (of which 1g saturates), 56g carbohydrate, 0.8g salt • Vegetarian • Easy

4 baking potatoes
1 tbsp olive oil, plus extra to rub
1 tsp smoked paprika, plus a pinch
2 shallots, finely chopped
1 tbsp freshly chopped rosemary
400g can cannellini beans, drained and rinsed
400g can chopped tomatoes
1 tbsp light muscovado sugar
1 tsp vegetarian Worcestershire sauce
75ml (2½fl oz) red wine
75ml (2½fl oz) hot vegetable stock

a small handful of freshly chopped flat-leafed parsley
grated mature vegetarian Cheddar to sprinkle
sea salt and ground black pepper

1. Preheat the oven to 200°C (180°C fan oven) mark 6. Rub the potatoes with a little oil and put them on a baking tray. Scatter with sea salt and a pinch of smoked paprika. Bake for 1–1½ hours.

2. Meanwhile, heat 1 tbsp oil in a large pan, then fry the shallots over a low heat for 1–2 minutes until they start to soften.

3. Add the rosemary and 1 tsp paprika and fry for 1–2 minutes, then add the beans, tomatoes, sugar, Worcestershire sauce, wine and hot stock. Season, then bring to the boil and simmer, uncovered, for 10–15 minutes. Serve with the baked potatoes, scattered with parsley and grated Cheddar.

TRY SOMETHING DIFFERENT
For a quick meal that takes less than 25 minutes, the spicy beans are just as good served with toast.

Baked Eggs

Preparation Time 10 minutes • Cooking Time 15 minutes • Serves 2 • Per Serving 238 calories, 21g fat (of which 5g saturates), 2g carbohydrate, 0.6g salt • Vegetarian • Easy

2 tbsp olive oil
125g (4oz) mushrooms, chopped
225g (8oz) fresh spinach
2 medium eggs
2 tbsp single cream
salt and ground black pepper

1. Preheat the oven to 200°C (180°C fan oven) mark 6. Heat the oil in a large frying pan, add the mushrooms and stir-fry for 30 seconds. Add the spinach and stir-fry until wilted. Season to taste, then divide the mixture between two shallow ovenproof dishes.

2. Carefully break an egg into the centre of each dish, then spoon 1 tbsp single cream over it.

3. Cook in the oven for about 12 minutes or until just set – the eggs will continue to cook a little once they're out of the oven. Grind a little more pepper over the top, if you like, and serve.

Mediterranean Kebabs

Preparation Time 15 minutes • Cooking Time 8–10 minutes • Serves 4 • Per Serving 164 calories, 13g fat (of which 5g saturates), 7g carbohydrate, 1.1g salt • Vegetarian • Easy

1 large courgette, cut into chunks
1 red pepper, seeded and cut into chunks
12 cherry tomatoes
125g (4oz) halloumi cheese, cubed
100g (3½oz) natural yogurt
1 tsp ground cumin
2 tbsp olive oil
squeeze of lemon
1 lemon, cut into eight wedges
couscous tossed with freshly chopped flat-leafed parsley to serve

1. Preheat the barbecue or grill. Soak eight wooden skewers in water for 20 minutes. Put the courgette into a large bowl with the red pepper, cherry tomatoes and halloumi cheese. Add the yogurt, cumin, oil and a squeeze of lemon and mix.

2. Push a lemon wedge on to each skewer, then divide the vegetables and cheese among the skewers. Grill the kebabs, turning regularly, for 8–10 minutes until the vegetables are tender and the halloumi is nicely charred. Serve with couscous.

Red Onions with Rosemary Dressing

Preparation Time 20 minutes • Cooking Time 30–35 minutes • Serves 8 • Per Serving 91 calories, 6g fat
(of which trace saturates), 9g carbohydrate, trace salt • Vegetarian • Easy

**3 large red onions, root intact,
each cut into eight wedges**
6 tbsp olive oil
4 tbsp balsamic vinegar
2 tsp freshly chopped rosemary
salt and ground black pepper

1. Preheat the barbecue. Soak eight wooden skewers in water for 20 minutes. Thread the onion wedges on to the skewers. Brush with about 3 tbsp oil, then season well with salt and pepper.

2. Barbecue the onion kebabs for 30–35 minutes, turning from time to time and brushing with oil when necessary, until tender and lightly charred.

3. To make the dressing, mix together the vinegar, the remaining oil and the rosemary. Drizzle the rosemary dressing over the cooked onions and serve.

Rösti Potatoes with Fried Eggs

Preparation Time 20 minutes, plus cooling • Cooking Time 20–25 minutes • Serves 4 • Per Serving 324 calories, 16g fat (of which 7g saturates), 36g carbohydrate, 0.4g salt • Vegetarian • A Little Effort

**900g (2lb) red potatoes, scrubbed
    and left whole**
40g (1½oz) butter
4 large eggs
salt and ground black pepper
**sprigs of flat-leafed parsley
    to garnish**

1. Put the potatoes into a large pan of cold water. Cover with a lid and bring to the boil, then parboil for 5–8 minutes. Drain and leave to cool for 15 minutes.

2. Preheat the oven to 150°C (130°C fan oven) mark 2. Put a baking tray inside to warm. Peel the potatoes and coarsely grate them lengthways into long strands. Divide into eight portions and shape into mounds.

3. Melt half the butter in a large non-stick frying pan. When it is beginning to brown, add four of the potato mounds, spacing them well apart, and flatten them a little. Fry slowly for 6–7 minutes until

golden brown, then turn them and brown the second side for 6–7 minutes. Transfer to a warmed baking tray and keep warm in the oven while you fry the rest.

4. Just before serving, carefully break the eggs into the hot pan and fry for about 2 minutes or until the white is set and the yolk is still soft. Season to taste with salt and pepper, and serve at once, with the rösti. Garnish with sprigs of parsley.

Bubble & Squeak Cakes

Preparation Time 15 minutes • Cooking Time 45 minutes, plus cooling • Makes 12 • Per Cake 130 calories, 10g fat (of which 6g saturates), 10g carbohydrate, 0.2g salt • Vegetarian • Easy

550g (1¼lb) old potatoes, peeled
125g (4oz) butter
175g (6oz) leeks, trimmed and finely shredded
175g (6oz) green cabbage, finely shredded
plain flour to dust
1 tbsp oil
salt and ground black pepper

1. Cook the potatoes in a large pan of lightly salted boiling water until tender, then drain and mash.

2. Heat 50g (2oz) butter in a large non-stick frying pan. Add the leeks and cabbage, and fry for 5 minutes, stirring, or until soft and beginning to colour. Combine the leeks and cabbage with the potatoes and season well with salt and pepper. Leave to cool. When cool enough to handle, mould into 12 cakes and dust with flour.

3. Heat the oil and remaining butter in a non-stick frying pan and cook the cakes for 4 minutes on each side or until they are golden crisp and hot right through. Serve.

Grilled Sweet Potatoes with Feta & Olives

Preparation Time 15 minutes • Cooking Time 15–20 minutes • Serves 4 • Per Serving 324 calories, 23g fat (of which 9g saturates), 21g carbohydrate, 2.5g salt • Vegetarian • Easy

1 large sweet potato, weighing about 500g (1lb 2oz)

4 tbsp olive oil, plus extra to brush

200g (7oz) feta cheese

2 tsp dried Herbes de Provence (see Cook's Tip)

50g (2oz) pitted black olives, chopped

1 garlic clove, crushed

salt and ground black pepper

flat-leafed parsley sprigs to garnish

1. Preheat the barbecue or griddle. Peel the sweet potato and cut lengthways into eight wedges. Put them into a pan of boiling water and bring back to the boil, then reduce the heat and simmer for 3 minutes. Drain and refresh in cold water. Drain, dry well on kitchen paper, then brush lightly with oil. Season with salt and pepper, then barbecue or grill for 10–15 minutes until well browned and cooked through.

2. Meanwhile, mash the cheese, herbs, olives, garlic and 4 tbsp oil together. Serve the sweet potato with the feta cheese mixture, garnished with flat-leafed parsley.

COOK'S TIPS

• *Herbes de Provence, an aromatic dried mixture made up of rosemary, thyme, basil, bay and savory, is a wonderful complement to barbecued or grilled food.*

• *For an authentic Mediterranean flavour, mix Herbes de Provence with olive oil and brush over chicken or lamb, then rub with coarse salt before grilling.*

Grilled Vegetables with Walnut Sauce

Preparation Time 25 minutes • Cooking Time 15–20 minutes • Serves 4 • Per Serving 598 calories, 48g fat (of which 6g saturates), 35g carbohydrate, 0.3g salt • Vegetarian • Easy

2 large carrots, peeled
1 fennel bulb
225g (8oz) sweet potatoes
225g (8oz) Jerusalem artichokes, scrubbed
225g (8oz) thick asparagus spears
8 baby leeks
4–6 tbsp olive oil
salt and ground black pepper

FOR THE WALNUT SAUCE
50g (2oz) day-old bread, crusts removed
75g (3oz) walnuts, toasted
2 garlic cloves, chopped
1 tbsp red wine vinegar
2 tbsp chopped parsley
90ml (3fl oz) olive oil
50ml (2fl oz) walnut oil

1. First make the walnut sauce. Crumble the bread into a bowl, add 2 tbsp water, then squeeze dry. Put the bread into a food processor with the toasted walnuts, garlic, wine vinegar and parsley, and blend until fairly smooth. Add the olive and walnut oils and process briefly to form a thick sauce. Season with salt and pepper and transfer to a serving dish.

2. Preheat the grill to medium-high. Prepare the vegetables. Cut the carrots into 5mm (¼in) slices; thinly slice the fennel lengthways; peel and thinly slice the sweet potatoes; thinly slice the Jerusalem artichokes. Trim the asparagus and leeks, but leave whole.

3. Baste the vegetables with olive oil and grill in batches, turning once, for 2–6 minutes on each side until charred and tender (see Cook's Tip); keep warm in a low oven while grilling the rest.

4. Transfer all the grilled vegetables to a warmed serving plate and season with a little salt and pepper. Serve accompanied by the walnut sauce.

COOK'S TIP
The root vegetables take longest to cook through, while the asparagus and leeks only need a short time under the grill.

Roasted Ratatouille

Preparation Time 15 minutes • Cooking Time 1½ hours • Serves 6 • Per Serving 224 calories, 18g fat (of which 3g saturates), 14g carbohydrate, 0g salt • Vegetarian • Easy

400g (14oz) red peppers, seeded
    and roughly chopped
700g (1½lb) aubergines, stalk
    removed, cut into chunks
450g (1lb) onions, peeled and
    cut into wedges
4 or 5 garlic cloves, unpeeled
    and left whole
150ml (¼ pint) olive oil
1 tsp fennel seeds
200ml (7fl oz) passata
sea salt and ground black pepper
a few fresh thyme sprigs to garnish

1. Preheat the oven to 240°C (220°C fan oven) mark 9. Put the peppers, aubergine, onions, garlic, olive oil and fennel seeds into a roasting tin. Season with sea salt flakes and pepper, and toss together.

2. Transfer to the oven and cook for 30 minutes, tossing frequently during cooking, or until the vegetables are charred and beginning to soften.

3. Stir the passata through the vegetables and put the roasting tin back in the oven for 50–60 minutes, stirring occasionally. Garnish with the thyme sprigs and serve.

TRY SOMETHING DIFFERENT
Replace half the aubergines with 400g (14oz) courgettes; use a mix of green and red peppers; garnish with fresh basil instead of thyme.

Baked Tomatoes & Fennel

Preparation Time 10 minutes • Cooking Time 1¼ hours • Serves 6 • Per Serving 127 calories, 9g fat
(of which 1g saturates), 7g carbohydrate, 0.1g salt • Vegetarian • Easy

**900g (2lb) fennel, trimmed and
cut into quarters**
75ml (2½fl oz) white wine
5 thyme sprigs
75ml (2½fl oz) olive oil
**900g (2lb) ripe beef or plum
tomatoes**

1. Preheat the oven to 200°C
(180°C fan oven) mark 6. Put the
fennel into a roasting tin and pour
the white wine over it. Snip the
thyme sprigs over the fennel,
drizzle with the oil and season.
Roast for 45 minutes.

2. Halve the tomatoes, add to
the roasting tin and continue
to roast for 30 minutes or until
tender, basting with the juices
halfway through.

COOK'S TIP
*This is an ideal accompaniment
to grilled fish or meat, or a
vegetarian frittata.*

Baked Potatoes with Mustard Seeds

Preparation Time 15–20 minutes • Cooking Time 1¼ hours • Serves 6 • Per Serving 315 calories, 17g fat (of which 9g saturates), 38g carbohydrate, 1g salt • Vegetarian • Easy

6 baking potatoes, about 1.4kg (3lb), scrubbed
2 tbsp sunflower oil
1 tbsp coarse sea salt
4–5 large garlic cloves, unpeeled
50g (2oz) butter
6 tbsp crème fraîche
2 tbsp mustard seeds, toasted and lightly crushed
salt and ground black pepper
fresh oregano sprigs to garnish

1. Preheat the oven to 200°C (180°C fan oven) mark 6. Prick the potato skins all over with a fork, rub with oil and sprinkle with salt. Cook in the oven for 1 hour. Twenty minutes before the end of the cooking time, put the garlic cloves in a small roasting tin and cook for 20 minutes.

2. Squeeze the potatoes gently to check they are well cooked, then remove the potatoes and garlic from the oven and leave to cool slightly. When cool enough to handle, slice the tops off the potatoes and scoop the flesh into a warm bowl. Squeeze the garlic out of its skin and add it to the potato flesh with the butter, crème fraîche and mustard seeds. Season to taste with salt and pepper, then mash well. Return the potato mixture to the hollowed skins.

3. Put the filled potatoes on a baking sheet and return to the oven for 15 minutes or until golden brown. Garnish with oregano sprigs and serve hot.

FREEZING TIP
To freeze *Complete the recipe to the end of step 2, then cool, wrap and freeze for up to one month.*
To use *Thaw overnight at cool room temperature. Cook at 200°C (180°C fan oven) mark 6 for 20–25 minutes or until piping hot to the centre.*

Roasted Potatoes & Parsnips

Preparation time 25 minutes • Cooking Time about 1 hour • Serves 8 • Per Serving 251 calories, 8g fat (of which 3g saturates), 43g carbohydrate, 1.9g salt • Easy

1.4kg (3lb) small, even-sized potatoes, scrubbed
800g (1lb 12oz) small parsnips, peeled
50g (2oz) goose fat
1–2 tbsp black mustard seeds
1 tbsp sea salt

1. Cut out small wedges from one side of each of the potatoes and parsnips (this will help make them extra crispy). Put them into a pan of lightly salted cold water, bring to the boil and cook for 6 minutes. Drain well.

2. Preheat the oven to 200°C (180°C fan oven) mark 6. Heat the goose fat in a roasting tin for 4–5 minutes until sizzling hot. Add the potatoes, toss well in the fat and roast for 30 minutes. Add the parsnips and sprinkle with the mustard seeds and sea salt.

3. Roast the vegetables for a further 30–35 minutes turning after 20 minutes, until golden.

FREEZING TIP
To freeze Complete the recipe to the end of step 1. Spread out the vegetables on a baking tray and leave to cool, then freeze on the tray. Once frozen, put them into a plastic bag and freeze for up to three months.
To use Cook from frozen, allowing an additional 15–20 minutes total cooking time.

Roasted Rosemary Potatoes

Preparation Time 10 minutes • Cooking Time 20–25 minutes • Serves 8 • Per Serving 102 calories, 4g fat
(of which 1g saturates), 15g carbohydrate, trace salt • Vegetarian • Easy

**750g (1lb 10oz) new potatoes,
   unpeeled**
3 tbsp olive oil
**8 rosemary stalks, each about
   18cm (7in) long**
salt and ground black pepper

1. Preheat the barbecue or grill. Cook the potatoes in lightly salted boiling water for 10 minutes or until nearly tender. Drain, cool a little, then toss in the oil. Season well. Strip most of the leaves from the rosemary stalks, leaving a few at the tip; set the stripped leaves to one side.

2. Thread the potatoes on to the rosemary stalks, place on the barbecue or grill and scatter with the leaves. Cook for 10–15 minutes, turning from time to time, until tender and lightly charred.

COOK'S TIP
Skewering the potatoes helps them to cook more quickly and makes them easier to handle on a barbecue. Using rosemary stalks adds a wonderful flavour.

Spicy Squash Quarters

Preparation Time 10 minutes • Cooking Time 20–30 minutes • Serves 8 • Per Serving 97 calories, 8g fat (of which 5g saturates), 4g carbohydrate, 0.1g salt • Vegetarian • Easy

2 small butternut squash, quartered and seeds discarded
75g (3oz) butter, melted
4 tsp peppered steak seasoning
coarse sea salt to sprinkle
wild rocket to serve

1. Preheat the grill or barbecue to medium-hot. Sprinkle the squash with sea salt, brush with butter and sprinkle the steak seasoning over.

2. Cook the squash quarters for 20–30 minutes until tender, turning them over occasionally. Serve hot, with wild rocket.

TRY SOMETHING DIFFERENT
Instead of the steak seasoning, lightly toast 2 tsp coriander seeds. Roughly crush and stir into the melted butter before brushing on to the squash. When cooked, toss with fresh coriander leaves.

Asparagus & Mangetouts with Lemon Sauce

Preparation Time 5–10 minutes • Cooking Time 10 minutes • Serves 4 • Per Serving 114 calories, 6g fat (of which 1g saturates), 10g carbohydrate, 0g salt • Vegetarian • Easy

225g (8oz) asparagus spears, trimmed and cut diagonally into three pieces
1 tbsp sesame seeds
1 tbsp vegetable oil
1 tsp sesame oil
225g (8oz) mangetouts
1 garlic clove, crushed
2 tbsp dry sherry
1 tbsp caster sugar
2 tsp light soy sauce
grated zest and juice of 1 lemon
1 tsp cornflour
salt
strips of lemon zest to garnish

1. Cook the asparagus in a pan of boiling salted water for 5 minutes or until just tender. Drain well.

2. Meanwhile, toast the sesame seeds in a hot wok or large frying pan until golden. Tip on to a plate.

3. Return the wok or frying pan to the heat and add the vegetable and sesame oils. Add the mangetouts, garlic and asparagus and stir-fry for 2 minutes.

4. Put the sherry, sugar, soy sauce, lemon zest and juice, cornflour and 5 tbsp water in a bowl and mix well.

5. Pour the mixture into the pan and cook, stirring, until the sauce thickens and coats the vegetables. Sprinkle with the toasted sesame seeds, garnish with lemon zest and serve immediately.

Courgettes with Sesame Seeds

Preparation Time 5 minutes • Cooking Time 12 minutes • Serves 6 • Per Serving 107 calories, 9g fat (of which 1g saturates), 3g carbohydrate, 0.4g salt • Vegetarian • Easy

2 tbsp sesame seeds

2 tbsp vegetable oil

4 garlic cloves, crushed

900g (2lb) courgettes, thinly sliced

1 spring onion, thickly sliced

½ tsp salt

1 tbsp sesame oil

ground black pepper

banana leaves to serve (optional, see Cook's Tip)

1. Toast the sesame seeds in a hot wok or large frying pan until golden. Tip on to a plate.

2. Heat the vegetable oil in the wok or frying pan. Add the garlic and fry for 2 minutes.

3. Add the courgettes and stir-fry for 7–8 minutes. Stir in the spring onion, salt and sesame oil. Season to taste with pepper. Cook for a further 1 minute, then add the toasted sesame seeds. Stir once and serve hot or cold on a bed of banana leaves, if you like.

COOK'S TIP

Banana leaves are sometimes used instead of plates in South-east Asia; they make an unusual presentation and are available from some Asian food shops.

Stir-fried Beans & Cherry Tomatoes

Preparation Time 10 minutes • Cooking Time about 8 minutes • Serves 6 • Per Serving 30 calories, 2g fat
(of which trace saturates), 3g carbohydrate, 0.1g salt • Vegetarian • Easy

350g (12oz) green beans, trimmed
2 tsp olive oil
1 large garlic clove, crushed
150g (5oz) cherry or baby plum tomatoes, halved
2 tbsp freshly chopped flat-leafed parsley
salt and ground black pepper

1. Cook the beans in boiling salted water for 4–5 minutes, then drain well.

2. Heat the oil in a wok or large frying pan over a high heat. Stir-fry the beans with the garlic and tomatoes for 2–3 minutes until the beans are tender and the tomatoes are just beginning to soften without losing their shape. Season well with salt and pepper, stir in the parsley and serve.

Stir-fried Green Vegetables

Preparation Time 5 minutes • Cooking Time 3–4 minutes • Serves 6 • Per Serving 100 calories, 8g fat (of which 3g saturates), 5g carbohydrate, 0.1g salt • Vegetarian • Easy

2 tbsp vegetable oil
225g (8oz) courgettes, thinly sliced
175g (6oz) mangetouts
25g (1oz) butter
175g (6oz) frozen peas, thawed
salt and ground black pepper

1. Heat the oil in a wok or large frying pan, add the courgettes and stir-fry for 1–2 minutes. Add the mangetouts and cook for 1 minute.

2. Add the butter and peas, and cook for 1 minute. Season to taste with salt and pepper and serve the vegetables immediately.

TRY SOMETHING DIFFERENT
Try other vegetables, such as thinly sliced leeks, spring onions or pak choi.

PUDDINGS

Classic Apple Pie

Preparation Time 20 minutes • Cooking Time 35–40 minutes • Serves 6 • Per Serving 268 calories, 11g fat (of which 4g saturates), 43g carbohydrate, 0.4g salt • Vegetarian • Easy

900g (2lb) cooking apples, peeled, cored and sliced
50g (2oz) caster sugar, plus extra to dust
Shortcrust Pastry (see Cook's Tip), made with 225g (8oz) plain flour, a pinch of salt, 100g (3½oz) chilled butter and 1 large egg
flour to dust

1. Preheat the oven to 190°C (170°C fan oven) mark 5.

2. Layer the apples and sugar in a 1.1 litre (2 pint) pie dish. Sprinkle with 1 tbsp water.

3. Roll out the pastry on a lightly floured surface to a circle 2.5cm (1in) larger than the pie dish. Cut off a strip the width of the rim of the dish, dampen the rim of the dish and press on the strip. Dampen the pastry strip and cover with the pastry circle, pressing the edges together well. Decorate the edge of the pastry and make a slit in the centre to allow steam to escape.

4. Bake for 35–40 minutes until the pastry is lightly browned. Sprinkle with caster sugar before serving.

COOK'S TIP
Shortcrust Pastry
This is a basic recipe for shortcrust pastry. Adjust the quantities of ingredients as specified in individual recipes.
Sift 125g (4oz) plain flour and a pinch of salt into a bowl and add 50g (2oz) chilled unsalted butter, cut into small pieces. Using your fingertips or a pastry cutter, rub or cut the butter into the flour until the mixture resembles fine breadcrumbs. Using a fork, mix in 1 medium egg yolk and 1½ tsp water until the mixture holds together; add a little more water if necessary. Knead lightly to form a firm dough. Gather the dough in your hands and lightly knead. Form the pastry into a ball, wrap tightly in clingfilm and chill for at least 1 hour before using. (This allows the pastry to 'relax' and prevents shrinkage when it is baked.) Makes 125g (4oz) pastry.

Rustic Blackberry & Apple Pie

Preparation Time 25 minutes, plus chilling • Cooking Time 40 minutes • Serves 6 • Per Serving 372 calories, 19g fat (of which 11g saturates), 49g carbohydrate, 0.4g salt • Vegetarian • Easy

200g (7oz) plain flour, plus
    extra to dust
125g (4oz) chilled unsalted
    butter, diced, plus extra
    to grease
1 medium egg, beaten
75g (3oz) golden caster sugar,
    plus 3 tbsp
a pinch of salt
500g (1lb 2oz) eating apples,
    quartered, cored and cut into
    chunky wedges
300g (11oz) blackberries
¼ tsp ground cinnamon
juice of 1 small lemon

1. Pulse the flour and butter in a food processor until it resembles coarse crumbs. (Alternatively, rub the butter into the flour by hand or using a pastry cutter.) Add the egg, 2 tbsp sugar and the salt, and pulse again to combine, or stir in. Wrap in clingfilm and chill for at least 15 minutes. Meanwhile, preheat the oven to 200°C (180°C fan oven) mark 6.

2. Put the apples, blackberries, 75g (3oz) sugar, the cinnamon and lemon juice in a bowl and toss together, making sure the sugar dissolves in the juice.

3. Grease a 25.5cm (10in) enamel or metal pie dish. Using a lightly floured rolling pin, roll out the pastry on a large sheet of baking parchment to a 30.5cm (12in) circle. Lift up the paper, upturn the pastry on to the pie dish and peel away the paper.

4. Put the prepared fruit in the centre of the pie dish and fold the pastry edges up and over the fruit. Sprinkle with the remaining sugar and bake for 40 minutes or until the fruit is tender and the pastry golden.

Rhubarb & Cinnamon Pie

Preparation Time 15 minutes, plus chilling • Cooking Time 50 minutes • Serves 6 • Per Serving 379 calories, 14g fat (of which 11g saturates), 55g carbohydrate, 0.3g salt • Vegetarian • Easy

- **175g (6oz) plain flour, plus extra to dust**
- **125g (4oz) butter, plus extra to grease**
- **150g (5oz) golden caster sugar**
- **700g (1½lb) rhubarb, cut into bite-size chunks**
- **2 tbsp cornflour**
- **½ tsp ground cinnamon**
- **a little milk and sugar to glaze**

1. Put the flour, butter and 25g (1oz) sugar into a food processor and whiz until the pastry comes together. (Alternatively, rub the butter into the flour in a large bowl by hand until it resembles fine crumbs. Stir in the sugar. Bring together and knead very briefly to form a ball.) If the dough is slightly sticky, roll it in some flour; chill for 20 minutes. Grease a 23cm (9in) round ovenproof dish with sides at least 5cm (2in) deep. Roll out the pastry on a lightly floured surface to a large circle, leaving the edges uneven. It should be large enough to line the dish and to allow the edges of the pastry to drape over the sides.

2. Preheat the oven to 200°C (180°C fan oven) mark 6. Toss the rhubarb in the remaining sugar, cornflour and cinnamon, and spoon into the dish. Bring the pastry edges up and over the fruit, leaving a gap in the centre. Glaze with milk and sprinkle with sugar.

3. Put on a baking sheet and bake for 50 minutes or until the pastry is golden brown and the juice is bubbling up. Serve hot.

TRY SOMETHING DIFFERENT
Add the grated zest of 1 orange instead of the cinnamon.

Plum & Cardamom Pie

Preparation Time 15 minutes • Cooking Time 30 minutes, plus 30 minutes cooling • Serves 6 • Per Serving
275 calories, 12g fat (of which 4g saturates), 41g carbohydrate, 0.4g salt • Vegetarian • Easy

250g (9oz) ready-rolled sweet shortcrust pastry
flour to dust
900g (2lb) mixed yellow and red plums, halved, stoned and quartered
2–3 green cardamom pods, split open, seeds removed and crushed or chopped
50–75g (2–3oz) caster sugar, plus extra to sprinkle
beaten egg or milk to glaze

1. Heat a flat baking sheet in the oven at 220°C (200°C fan oven) mark 7. Roll out the pastry on a lightly floured surface a little thinner into a 30.5cm (12in) circle. Put it on a floured baking sheet, without a lip if possible.

2. Pile the fruit on to the pastry and sprinkle with the cardamom seeds and sugar (if the plums are tart you'll need all of it; less if they are ripe and sweet). Fold in the pastry edges and pleat together.

3. Brush the pastry with beaten egg or milk and sprinkle with sugar. Put on the preheated sheet and bake for 30 minutes until the pastry is golden brown and the plums are just tender. The juices will begin to bubble from the pie as it cooks.

4. Leave to cool for 10 minutes, then carefully loosen the pastry around the edges. Cool for another 20 minutes, then transfer very carefully to a serving plate. Sprinkle with a little sugar and serve warm.

TRY SOMETHING DIFFERENT
Replace the plums with pears, toss them in a little lemon juice, and sprinkle with ½ tsp cinnamon instead of the cardamom.

Sugar-crusted Fruit Pie

Preparation Time 30 minutes, plus 30 minutes chilling • Cooking Time about 40 minutes • Serves 4 •
Per Serving 673 calories, 38g fat (of which 17g saturates), 79g carbohydrate, 0.5g salt • Vegetarian • Easy

75g (3oz) hazelnuts
350g (12oz) cherries, stoned
75g (3oz) caster sugar, plus 2 tbsp
175g (6oz) plain flour, plus extra
    to dust
125g (4oz) butter
275g (10oz) cooking apples, peeled,
    cored and quartered

1. Spread the hazelnuts over a baking sheet. Toast under a hot grill until golden brown, turning them frequently. Put the hazelnuts in a clean teatowel and rub off the skins. Leave to cool.

2. Put the cherries into a bowl with 25g (1oz) caster sugar. Cover and set aside. For the hazelnut pastry, put 50g (2oz) hazelnuts into a food processor with the flour and pulse to a powder. Remove and set aside. In the food processor, whiz the butter with 50g (2oz) sugar. Add the flour mixture and pulse until it forms a dough. Turn out on to a lightly floured surface and knead lightly, then wrap and chill for 30 minutes. If the pastry cracks, just work it together.

3. Preheat the oven to 180°C (160°C fan oven) mark 4. Cut the apples into small chunks and put into a 900ml (1½ pint) oval pie dish. Spoon the cherries on top. Roll out the pastry on a lightly floured surface to about 5mm (¼in) thick. Cut into 1cm (½in) strips. Dampen the edge of the pie dish with a little water and press a few of the strips on to the rim to cover it.

Dampen the pastry rim. Put the remaining strips over the cherries to create a lattice pattern.

4. Brush the pastry with water and sprinkle with the extra sugar. Bake for 30–35 minutes until the pastry is golden. Set aside to cool for 15 minutes.

5. Chop the remaining toasted hazelnuts and sprinkle over the tart. Serve warm.

GET AHEAD
To prepare ahead Complete the recipe to the end of step 4, then cool, wrap and chill for up to three days.
To use Bake at 180°C (160°C fan oven) mark 4 for 20–25 minutes to heat through. Complete the recipe.

FREEZING TIP
To freeze Complete the recipe to the end of step 3, then wrap and freeze.
To use Brush the pastry with egg and sprinkle the extra sugar on top. Bake from frozen at 180°C (160°C fan oven) mark 4 for 40–45 minutes until golden. Complete the recipe.

Baked Raspberry Meringue Pie

Preparation time 15 minutes • Cooking time 8 minutes • Serves 8 • Per Serving 176 calories, 2g fat (of which 1g saturates), 37g carbohydrate, 0.1g salt • Vegetarian • Easy

8 trifle sponges
450g (1lb) raspberries, lightly crushed
2–3 tbsp raspberry liqueur
3 medium egg whites
150g (5oz) golden caster sugar

1. Preheat the oven to 230°C (210°C fan oven) mark 8. Put the trifle sponges into the bottom of a 2 litre (3½ pint) ovenproof dish. Spread the raspberries on top and drizzle with the raspberry liqueur.

2. Whisk the egg whites in a clean grease-free bowl until stiff peaks form. Gradually whisk in the sugar until the mixture is smooth and glossy. Spoon the meringue mixture over the raspberries and bake for 6–8 minutes until golden.

Lemon Meringue Pie

Preparation Time 30 minutes • Cooking Time about 1 hour, plus standing • Serves 8 • Per Serving 692 calories, 36g fat (of which 21g saturates), 83g carbohydrate, 0.6g salt • Vegetarian • Easy

23cm (9in) ready-made sweet
    pastry case

FOR THE FILLING
**7 medium eggs, 4 separated,
    at room temperature**
finely grated zest of 3 lemons
**175ml (6fl oz) freshly squeezed
    lemon juice (about 4 lemons),
    strained**
400g can condensed milk
150ml (¼ pint) double cream
225g (8oz) golden icing sugar

1. Preheat the oven to 180°C (160°C fan oven) mark 4. To make the filling, put 4 egg yolks into a bowl with the 3 whole eggs. Add the lemon zest and juice and whisk lightly. Mix in the condensed milk and cream.

2. Pour the filling into the pastry case and bake for 30 minutes or until just set in the centre. Put to one side to cool while you prepare the meringue. Increase the oven temperature to 200°C (180°C fan oven) mark 6.

3. For the meringue, whisk the egg whites and sugar together in a heatproof bowl set over a pan of gently simmering water, using a hand-held electric whisk, for 10 minutes or until very shiny and thick. Remove from the heat and whisk at a low speed for a further 5–10 minutes until the bowl is cool.

4. Pile the meringue on top of the lemon filling and swirl with a palette knife to form peaks. Bake for 5–10 minutes until the meringue is tinged brown. Leave to stand for about 1 hour, then serve.

Pecan Pie

Preparation Time 25 minutes, plus chilling • Cooking Time 1 hour 10 minutes, plus cooling • Serves 8 •
Per Serving 549 calories, 40g fat (of which 16g saturates), 45g carbohydrate, 0.4g salt • Vegetarian • Easy

Sweet Shortcrust Pastry (see Cook's Tip) made with 175g (6oz) plain flour, 75g (3oz) chilled butter, 50g (2oz) icing sugar and 1 medium egg
flour to dust
ice cream to serve

FOR THE FILLING
125g (4oz) butter
4 tbsp clear honey
25g (1oz) caster sugar
75g (3oz) dark soft brown sugar
3 tbsp double cream
grated zest of 1 small lemon
1 tsp vanilla extract
175g (6oz) pecan nuts

1. Roll the shortcrust pastry on a lightly floured surface into a 30.5cm (12in) diameter circle and use to line a 20.5cm (8in) diameter, 2.5cm (1in) deep, loose-based fluted tart tin. Put the tin on a baking sheet and chill for 20 minutes. Meanwhile, preheat the oven to 200°C (180°C fan oven) mark 6. Line the pastry case with greaseproof paper and baking beans, and bake for 15 minutes. Remove the paper and beans, then return the pastry case to the oven for a further 10 minutes. Reduce the oven temperature to 150°C (130°C fan oven) mark 2.

2. To make the filling, melt the butter with the honey and sugars over a low heat, bring to the boil without stirring and bubble for 2–3 minutes. Remove from the heat, stir in the cream, lemon zest, vanilla extract and nuts, and leave to cool for 15 minutes.

3. Pour the pecan mixture into the pastry case. Bake for 40 minutes or until the mixture begins to bubble in the middle (cover with foil if it gets too dark). Serve warm with ice cream.

COOK'S TIP
Sweet Shortcrust Pastry
This is a basic recipe for shortcrust pastry. Adjust the quantities of ingredients as specified in individual recipes.
Sift 125g (4oz) plain flour and a pinch of salt into a bowl and add 50g (2oz) unsalted butter, cut into small pieces. Using your fingertips or a pastry cutter, rub or cut the butter into the flour until the mixture resembles fine breadcrumbs. Using a fork, mix in 50g (2oz) caster sugar, 2 medium egg yolks and 1½ tsp water until the mixture holds together; add a little more water if necessary. Gather the dough in your hands and knead lightly. Form into a ball, wrap tightly in clingfilm and chill for at least 30 minutes before using. (This 'relaxes' the pastry and prevents shrinkage when it is baked.) Makes 125g (4oz) pastry.

GET AHEAD
To prepare ahead Complete the recipe then cool and store in an airtight container for up to two days.
To use Heat the pie at 180°C (160°C fan oven) mark 4 for 15–20 minutes.
To freeze Complete the recipe then cool, wrap and freeze the pie in its tin.
To use Reheat the pie from frozen at 180°C (160°C fan oven) mark 4 for 25 minutes or until warm. Cover with foil if it gets too dark.

American-style Plum Cobbler

Preparation Time 25 minutes • Cooking Time 40 minutes • Serves 6 • Per Serving 451 calories, 15g fat (of which 9g saturates), 76g carbohydrate, 0.3g salt • Vegetarian • Easy

900g (2lb) plums, halved and stoned
150g (5oz) golden caster sugar, plus 3 tbsp
1 tbsp cornflour
250g (9oz) self-raising flour
100g (3½oz) chilled unsalted butter, diced
175ml (6fl oz) buttermilk or whole natural yogurt

1. Preheat the oven to 200°C (180°C fan oven) mark 6. Cut the plums into chunky wedges. Tip into an ovenproof dish measuring 25.5 × 18 × 7.5cm (10 × 7 × 3in) and toss together with 3 tbsp sugar and the cornflour.

2. Whiz the flour, butter and 100g (3½oz) sugar in a food processor until the mixture forms fine crumbs. (Alternatively, rub the fat into the flour by hand or using a pastry cutter, then stir in the sugar.) Add the buttermilk or

yogurt and blend for a few seconds until just combined.

3. Scatter clumps of the dough over the plums, leaving some of the fruit exposed. Sprinkle the cobbler with the remaining sugar and bake for 40 minutes or until the fruit is tender and the topping is a pale golden brown.

TRY SOMETHING DIFFERENT
Toss the plums with the grated zest of ½ orange before baking, and add the grated zest of the remaining ½ orange to the cobbler mixture with the buttermilk.

Pear & Blackberry Crumble

Preparation Time 20 minutes • Cooking Time 35–45 minutes • Serves 6 • Per Serving 525 calories, 21g fat (of which 9g saturates), 81g carbohydrate, 0.3g salt • Vegetarian • Easy

450g (1lb) pears, peeled, cored and chopped, tossed with the juice of 1 lemon
225g (8oz) golden caster sugar
1 tsp mixed spice
450g (1lb) blackberries
100g (3½oz) butter, chopped, plus extra to grease
225g (8oz) plain flour
75g (3oz) ground almonds
cream, custard or ice cream to serve

1. Put the pears and lemon juice into a bowl, add 100g (3½oz) sugar and the mixed spice, then add the blackberries and toss thoroughly to coat.

2. Preheat the oven to 200°C (180°C fan oven) mark 6. Lightly butter a 1.8 litre (3¼ pint) shallow dish, then carefully tip the fruit into the dish in an even layer.

3. Put the butter, flour, ground almonds and the remaining sugar into a food processor and pulse until the mixture begins to resemble breadcrumbs. Alternatively, rub the butter into the flour by hand or using a pastry cutter, then stir in the sugar. Tip into a bowl and bring parts of it together with your hands to make lumps. Spoon the crumble topping evenly over the fruit, then bake for 35–45 minutes until the fruit is tender and the crumble is golden and bubbling. Serve with cream, custard or ice cream.

TRY SOMETHING DIFFERENT
Use apples instead of pears.

Rhubarb & Orange Crumble Tart

Preparation Time 25 minutes, plus chilling • Cooking Time about 40 minutes, plus cooling • Cuts into 8 Slices •
Per Slice 518 calories, 37g fat (of which 22g saturates), 45g carbohydrate, 0.3g salt • Vegetarian • Easy

200g (7oz) plain flour, plus
    extra to dust
125g (4oz) unsalted butter,
    cut into small pieces
25g (1oz) golden caster sugar
cream to serve

FOR THE FILLING
550g (1¼lb) rhubarb, cut into
    2.5cm (1in) pieces
50g (2oz) golden caster sugar
grated zest of 1 orange
juice of ½ orange

**FOR THE CRUMBLE
TOPPING**
50g (2oz) plain flour
25g (1oz) ground almonds
50g (2oz) light muscovado sugar
25g (1oz) unsalted butter, cut into
    small pieces

1. To make the pastry, whiz the flour, butter and caster sugar in a food processor until it resembles fine crumbs. (Alternatively, rub the butter into the flour in a large bowl, by hand or using a pastry cutter, until it resembles fine crumbs. Stir in the sugar.) Add 2 tbsp cold water and whiz briefly again, or stir with a fork, to form a soft pastry. Wrap the pastry in clingfilm and chill for at least 30 minutes.

2. Roll out the pastry on a lightly floured worksurface and use to line a 10 × 35.5cm (4 × 14in) loose-based tin, or a 23cm (9in) round loose-based tart tin. Chill for 30 minutes. Preheat the oven to 200°C (180°C fan oven) mark 6. Bake the tart case blind (see page 218, step 1).

3. Meanwhile, make the filling. Put the rhubarb, caster sugar, orange zest and juice into a pan and bring to the boil. Cook gently for 6–8 minutes until the rhubarb has just softened. Allow to cool.

4. To make the crumble topping, put the flour, almonds, muscovado sugar and butter into the food processor and whiz briefly until it resembles fine crumbs. (Alternatively, rub the butter into the flour in a bowl, by hand or using a pastry cutter, until it resembles fine crumbs. Stir in the almonds and sugar.)

5. Spoon the rhubarb filling into the pastry case and level the surface. Top with the crumble mixture and bake for 20 minutes or until pale golden. Leave to cool slightly before serving with cream.

Treacle Tart

Preparation Time 25 minutes, plus chilling • Cooking Time 45–50 minutes, plus cooling • Serves 6 •
Per Serving 486 calories, 15g fat (of which 8g saturates), 88g carbohydrate, 1.1g salt • Vegetarian • Easy

**Sweet Shortcrust Pastry (see
Cook's Tip, page 234), made
with 225g (8oz) plain flour,
150g (5oz) unsalted butter,
15g (½oz) golden caster sugar
and 1 medium egg yolk**
flour to dust

FOR THE FILLING
700g (1½lb) golden syrup
175g (6oz) fresh white breadcrumbs
grated zest of 3 lemons
2 medium eggs, lightly beaten

1. Preheat the oven to 180°C
(160°C fan oven) mark 4. Roll out
the pastry on a lightly floured
surface and use to line a 25.5cm
(10in), 4cm (1½in) deep, loose-
based fluted tart tin. Prick the base
all over with a fork and chill for
30 minutes.

2. To make the filling, heat the
golden syrup in a pan over a low
heat until thinner in consistency.
Remove from the heat and mix in
the breadcrumbs and lemon zest.
Stir in the beaten eggs.

3. Pour the filling into the pastry
case and bake for 45–50 minutes
until the filling is lightly set and
golden. Allow to cool slightly.
Serve warm.

Easy Pear & Toffee Tarte Tatin

Preparation Time 15 minutes • Cooking Time 25–30 minutes, plus cooling • Cuts into 6 Slices • Per Slice
294 calories, 12g fat (of which 2g saturates), 46g carbohydrate, 0.5g salt • Vegetarian • Easy

**4 small, rosy pears, quartered and
cored – no need to peel them**
8 tbsp dulce de leche toffee sauce
225g (8oz) ready-rolled puff pastry
flour to dust
cream or vanilla ice cream to serve

1. Preheat the oven to 200°C (180°C fan oven) mark 6. Put the pears and toffee sauce into a large non-stick frying pan. Cook over a medium heat for 5 minutes or until the pears are well coated and the sauce has turned a slightly darker shade of golden brown.

2. Tip the pears and sauce into a 20.5cm (8in) non-stick sandwich or tart tin. Arrange the pears, skin side down, in a circle and leave to cool for 10 minutes.

3. If necessary, roll out the puff pastry on a lightly floured surface until it is wide enough to cover the tin. Lay it over the pears and press down on to the edge of the tin. Trim off any excess pastry. Prick the pastry all over, then bake for 20–25 minutes until well risen and golden.

4. Leave to cool for 5 minutes. To turn out, hold a large serving plate or baking sheet over the tart, turn over and give a quick shake to loosen. Lift off the tin. Serve the tart immediately, cut into wedges, with cream or ice cream.

TRY SOMETHING DIFFERENT
Replace the pears with 3–4 bananas, thickly sliced on the diagonal. Cook the dulce de leche for 5 minutes in step 1, stir in the bananas to coat, then arrange in the tin in an overlapping circle. Complete the recipe.

Rice Pudding

Preparation Time 5 minutes • Cooking Time 1½ hours • Serves 6 • Per Serving 239 calories, 8g fat (of which 5g saturates), 34g carbohydrate, 0.2g salt • Vegetarian • Easy

butter to grease
125g (4oz) short-grain pudding rice
1.1 litres (2 pints) whole (full-fat) milk
50g (2oz) golden caster sugar
1 tsp vanilla extract
grated zest of 1 orange (optional)
freshly grated nutmeg to taste

1. Preheat the oven to 170°C (150°C fan oven) mark 3. Lightly butter a 1.7 litre (3 pint) ovenproof dish. Add the rice, milk, sugar, vanilla extract and orange zest, if using, and stir everything together. Grate the nutmeg over the top of the mixture.

2. Bake the pudding in the middle of the oven for 1½ hours or until the top is golden brown.

Bread & Butter Pudding

Preparation Time 10 minutes, plus soaking • Cooking Time 30–40 minutes • Serves 4 • Per Serving 450 calories, 13g fat (of which 5g saturates), 70g carbohydrate, 1.1g salt • Vegetarian • Easy

50g (2oz) unsalted butter, softened, plus extra to grease
275g (10oz) white farmhouse bread, cut into 1cm (½in) slices, crusts removed
50g (2oz) raisins or sultanas
3 medium eggs
450ml (¾ pint) milk
3 tbsp golden icing sugar, plus extra to dust

1. Lightly butter four 300ml (½ pint) gratin dishes or one 1.1 litre (2 pint) ovenproof dish. Butter the bread, then cut into quarters to make triangles. Arrange the bread in the dish(es) and sprinkle with the raisins or sultanas.

2. Beat the eggs, milk and sugar in a bowl. Pour the mixture over the bread and leave to soak for 10 minutes. Preheat the oven to 180°C (160°C fan oven) mark 4.

3. Put the pudding(s) in the oven and bake for 30–40 minutes. Dust with icing sugar to serve.

Chocolate Bread Pudding

Preparation Time 20 minutes, plus chilling • Cooking Time 55 minutes–1¼ hours • Serves 6 • Per Serving
390 calories, 17g fat (of which 6g saturates), 51g carbohydrate, 0.7g salt • Vegetarian • A Little Effort

200g (7oz) baguette
100g (3½oz) milk chocolate,
   roughly chopped
500g carton fresh custard
150ml (¼ pint) semi-skimmed milk
1 large egg, beaten
butter to grease

1 tbsp demerara sugar
50g (2oz) walnuts, finely chopped
50g (2oz) plain or milk chocolate,
   in chunks
single cream to serve (optional)

1. Roughly chop the baguette and put it into a large bowl. Put the chopped milk chocolate into a pan with the custard and milk over a low heat. Stir gently until the chocolate has melted. Beat in the egg.

2. Pour the chocolate mixture over the bread, stir well to coat, then cover and chill for at least 4 hours.

3. Preheat the oven to 180°C (160°C fan oven) mark 4. Spoon the soaked bread into a buttered 1.4 litre (2½ pint), 7.5cm (3in) deep ovenproof dish, then bake for 30–40 minutes.

4. Sprinkle with the sugar, walnuts and chocolate chunks. Put the dish back in the oven for 20–30 minutes until lightly set. Serve the pudding warm, with single cream if you like.

TRY SOMETHING DIFFERENT
Instead of baguette, use croissants or brioche for a richer pudding.

Panettone Pudding

Preparation Time 20 minutes, plus soaking • Cooking Time 35–45 minutes • Serves 6 • Per Serving 581 calories, 29g fat (of which 16g saturates), 73g carbohydrate, 0.9g salt • Vegetarian • Easy

- 50g (2oz) butter, at room temperature, plus extra to grease
- 500g (1lb 2oz) panettone (see Cook's Tip), cut into slices about 5mm (¼in) thick
- 3 large eggs, beaten
- 150g (5oz) golden caster sugar
- 300ml (½ pint) full-fat milk
- 150ml (¼ pint) double cream
- grated zest of 1 orange

1. Butter a 2 litre (3½ pint) ovenproof dish. Lightly butter the panettone slices, then tear them into pieces and arrange in the dish.

2. Mix the eggs with the sugar in a large bowl, then whisk in the milk, cream and orange zest. Pour the mixture over the buttered panettone and leave to soak for 20 minutes. Preheat the oven to 170°C (150°C fan oven) mark 3.

3. Put the dish in a roasting tin and pour in enough hot water to come halfway up the sides. Bake for 35–45 minutes until the pudding is just set in the middle and golden.

COOK'S TIP

Panettone is a yeasted fruit cake that is a traditional Christmas treat in Italy and is most widely available around Christmas time. If you can't find it, use brioche or cinnamon and raisin bread.

Cherry & Tangerine Sticky Puddings

Preparation Time 20 minutes, plus soaking • Cooking Time 25 minutes • Serves 8 • Per Serving 664 calories, 39g fat (of which 22g saturates), 79g carbohydrate, 0.7g salt • Vegetarian • Easy

about 25g (1oz) white vegetable
  fat, melted
200g (7oz) dried cherries
2 tbsp orange-flavoured liqueur
¾ tsp bicarbonate of soda
75g (3oz) unsalted butter, softened
150g (5oz) golden caster sugar
2 medium eggs, beaten
175g (6oz) self-raising flour

FOR THE SAUCE
175g (6oz) light muscovado sugar
125g (4oz) unsalted butter
6 tbsp double cream
25g (1oz) pecan nuts, chopped
juice of 1 tangerine

1. Preheat the oven to 180°C (160°C fan oven) mark 4. Using the melted fat, lightly oil eight 175ml (6fl oz) metal pudding basins or ramekins, then put a circle of non-stick baking parchment into the base of each.

2. Put 175g (6oz) dried cherries into a bowl and pour 150ml (¼ pint) boiling water over them. Stir in the liqueur and bicarbonate of soda, then leave to soak for 1 hour.

3. Whisk the butter and sugar in a large bowl until pale and fluffy, then beat in the eggs a little at a time. Fold in the cherry mixture.

4. Add the flour and fold in with a large metal spoon. Divide the mixture equally among the basins, then place on a baking sheet and bake for about 25 minutes or until well risen and firm.

5. Meanwhile, make the sauce. Put the sugar, butter, cream, pecan nuts and remaining cherries in a pan. Heat gently until the sugar has dissolved. Stir in the tangerine juice.

6. Leave the puddings to cool for 5 minutes, then turn out. Serve topped with the sauce.

FREEZING TIP
To freeze Cool the puddings completely. Wrap in clingfilm. Pour the sauce into a freezerproof container and leave to cool. Freeze both for up to one month.
To use Thaw the puddings and sauce overnight in the fridge. Warm the sauce. Meanwhile, put the puddings on a microwaveable plate. Spoon 1 tbsp sauce over each. Warm in the microwave on High for 2 minutes. Serve with the remaining sauce.

Steamed Syrup Sponge Puddings

Preparation Time 20 minutes • Cooking Time 35 minutes or 1½ hours • Serves 4 • Per Serving 580 calories, 29g fat (of which 17g saturates), 76g carbohydrate, 0.7g salt • Vegetarian • Easy

125g (4oz) unsalted butter, softened, plus extra to grease
3 tbsp golden syrup
125g (4oz) golden caster sugar
few drops of vanilla extract
2 medium eggs, beaten
175g (6oz) self-raising flour, sifted
about 3 tbsp milk
custard or cream to serve

1. Half-fill a steamer or large pan with water and put it on to boil. Grease four 300ml (½ pint) basins or a 900ml (1½ pint) pudding basin and spoon the syrup into the bottom.

2. Cream the butter and sugar together until pale and fluffy. Stir in the vanilla extract. Add the eggs a little at a time, beating well after each addition.

3. Using a metal spoon, fold in half the flour, then fold in the remaining flour with enough milk to give a dropping consistency. Spoon the mixture into the prepared pudding basin(s).

4. Cover with greased and pleated greaseproof paper and foil (see step 3, page 232), and secure with string. Steam for 35 minutes for individual puddings or 1½ hours for one large pudding, checking the water level from time to time and topping up with boiling water as necessary. Turn out on to warmed plates and serve with custard or cream.

TRY SOMETHING DIFFERENT
Instead of syrup, try the following.
Steamed Jam Sponge Puddings
Put 4 tbsp raspberry or blackberry jam into the base of the basins instead of the syrup.
Steamed Chocolate Sponge Puddings
Omit the golden syrup. Blend 4 tbsp cocoa powder with 2 tbsp hot water, then gradually beat into the creamed mixture before adding the eggs.

Pear & Ginger Steamed Pudding

Preparation Time 20 minutes • Cooking Time 1 hour 35 minutes • Serves 8 • Per Serving 314 calories, 14g fat (of which 9g saturates), 45g carbohydrate, 0.6g salt • Vegetarian • Easy

125g (4oz) unsalted butter, softened, plus extra to grease

1 large pear, peeled, cored and diced

2 tbsp golden caster sugar

2 balls stem ginger, finely chopped, plus 2 tbsp ginger syrup

4 tbsp golden syrup

125g (4oz) light muscovado sugar

finely grated zest of 1 lemon

2 medium eggs, beaten

175g (6oz) self-raising flour

2 tsp ground ginger

3 tbsp perry or pear juice

1. Grease a 900ml (1½ pint) pudding basin. Put the pear into a pan with 2 tbsp water and the caster sugar and simmer for 5 minutes. Stir in the stem ginger and the ginger and golden syrups and leave to cool. Tip into the basin.

2. Beat the butter, muscovado sugar and lemon zest in a bowl with a hand-held electric whisk until light and fluffy. Beat in the eggs a little at a time.

3. Fold in the flour and ground ginger, then fold in the perry or pear juice. Pour the mixture into the basin on top of the pear compote. Cut out a piece each of greaseproof paper and kitchen foil, each measuring 30.5 × 30.5cm (12 × 12in). Place the greaseproof on the foil and fold a pleat in the middle. Put on top of the pudding basin – it should overhang the sides. Tie the paper under the rim of the basin with string, using extra to make a knotted handle over the top. Trim off the excess paper and foil.

4. Sit the basin on an upturned saucer in a large pan. Pour in enough boiling water to come halfway up the basin. Cover and steam for 1¼–1½ hours, topping up with boiling water as necessary. Turn out on to a plate and serve.

Hot Pear & White Chocolate Puddings

Preparation Time 20 minutes • Cooking Time 20 minutes • Serves 4 • Per Serving 524 calories, 30g fat (of which 16g saturates), 61g carbohydrate, 0.5g salt • Vegetarian • Easy

100g (3½oz) butter, softened, plus extra to grease
100g (3½oz) self-raising flour, sifted
100g (3½oz) light muscovado sugar
1 tsp cocoa powder
1 medium egg
2–3 drops of almond extract
50g (2oz) white chocolate, chopped
2 ripe pears
25g (1oz) flaked almonds

1. Preheat the oven to 180°C (160°C fan oven) mark 4. Lightly grease four 250ml (9fl oz) ramekins.

2. Put half the butter, half the flour and half the muscovado sugar into a bowl. Add the cocoa powder, egg and almond extract and beat together until smooth. Divide the mixture among the prepared ramekins. Scatter half the chocolate on top.

3. Peel, core and chop the pears, then divide among the ramekins.

4. In a bowl, rub together the remaining butter, flour and sugar until the mixture resembles breadcrumbs. Stir in the flaked almonds and the remaining chocolate, then sprinkle over the pears and bake for 20 minutes or until golden. Serve hot.

Quick Gooey Chocolate Puddings

Preparation Time 15 minutes • Cooking Time 12–15 minutes • Serves 4 • Per Serving 468 calories, 31g fat (of which 19g saturates), 46g carbohydrate, 0.6g salt • Vegetarian • Easy

100g (3½oz) unsalted butter, plus extra to grease

100g (3½oz) golden caster sugar, plus extra to dust

100g (3½oz) plain chocolate (at least 70% cocoa solids), broken into pieces

2 large eggs

20g (¾oz) plain flour

icing sugar to dust

1. Preheat the oven to 200°C (180°C fan oven) mark 6. Butter four 200ml (7fl oz) ramekins and dust with sugar. Melt the chocolate and butter in a heatproof bowl set over a pan of gently simmering water, making sure the base of the bowl doesn't touch the water. Take the bowl off the pan and leave to cool for 5 minutes.

2. Whisk the eggs, caster sugar and flour together in a bowl until smooth. Fold in the chocolate mixture and pour into the ramekins.

3. Stand the dishes on a baking tray and bake for 12–15 minutes until the puddings are puffed and set on the outside, but still runny inside.

4. Turn out, dust with icing sugar and serve immediately.

Cinnamon Pancakes

Preparation Time 5 minutes • Cooking Time 20 minutes • Serves 6 • Per Serving 141 calories, 5g fat
(of which 1g saturates), 20g carbohydrate, 0.1g salt • Vegetarian • Easy

150g (5oz) plain flour
½ tsp ground cinnamon
1 medium egg
300ml (½ pint) skimmed milk
olive oil to fry
fruit compôte or sugar and Greek
  yogurt to serve

1. In a large bowl, whisk together the flour, cinnamon, egg and milk to make a smooth batter. Leave to stand for 20 minutes.

2. Heat a heavy-based frying pan over a medium heat. When the pan is really hot, add 1 tsp oil, pour in a ladleful of batter and tilt the pan to coat the base with an even layer. Cook for 1 minute or until golden. Flip over and cook for 1 minute.

Repeat with the remaining batter, adding more oil if necessary, to make six pancakes. Serve with a fruit compote or a sprinkling of sugar, and a dollop of yogurt.

TRY SOMETHING DIFFERENT
Serve with sliced bananas and vanilla ice cream instead of the fruit compote and yogurt.

Chocolate Crêpes with a Boozy Sauce

Preparation Time 5 minutes, plus standing • Cooking Time 10–15 minutes • Serves 4 • Per Serving 594 calories, 35g fat (of which 17g saturates), 57g carbohydrate, 0.5g salt • Vegetarian • Easy

100g (3½oz) plain flour, sifted

a pinch of salt

1 medium egg

300ml (½ pint) semi-skimmed milk

sunflower oil for frying

50g (2oz) plain chocolate (at least 70% cocoa solids), roughly chopped

100g (3½oz) unsalted butter

100g (3½oz) light muscovado sugar, plus extra to sprinkle

4 tbsp brandy

1. Put the flour and salt into a bowl, make a well in the centre and add the egg. Use a balloon whisk to mix the egg with a little of the flour, then gradually add the milk to make a smooth batter. Cover and leave to stand for about 20 minutes.

2. Pour the batter into a jug. Heat 1 tsp oil in a 23cm (9in) frying pan, then pour in 100ml (3½fl oz) batter, tilting the pan so that the mixture coats the base. Fry for 1–2 minutes until golden underneath. Turn carefully and fry the other side. Tip on to a plate, cover with a piece of greaseproof paper and repeat with the remaining batter, using more oil as needed.

3. Divide the chocolate among the crêpes. Fold each crêpe in half, and then in half again.

4. Put the butter and sugar into a heavy-based frying pan over a low heat. Add the brandy and stir. Slide the crêpes into the pan and cook for 3–4 minutes to melt the chocolate. Serve drizzled with sauce and sprinkled with sugar.

TRY SOMETHING DIFFERENT
Replace the brandy with Grand Marnier and use orange-flavoured plain chocolate.

Index